Finding FISH in a Strengths-Based Practice

Fulfilment, Inspiration, Success
and Happiness in a Life Well-Lived

Finding
FISH

in a Strengths-Based Practice

CHRISTOPHER
MILLER

Copyright © 2024 Christopher Miller

All rights reserved. No part of this publication may be reproduced, distributed, or transmitted in any form or by any means, including photocopying, recording, or other electronic or mechanical methods, without the prior written permission of the publisher, except in the case of brief quotations embodied in critical reviews and certain other noncommercial uses permitted by copyright law.

First published in 2024 by Hambone Publishing
Melbourne, Australia

The author (Christopher Miller) is happy to give permission for the contents of this book to be reproduced and distributed in any form that adds value to Practice Owners around the world, ideally with attribution to the author whenever appropriate. Ideally, any reproduction would include an element of improving on the principles shared here to create even greater impact.

Gallup®, CliftonStrengths® and the CliftonStrengths 34 Themes of Talent are trademarks of Gallup, Inc. All rights reserved. The non-Gallup® information you are receiving has not been approved and is not sanctioned or endorsed by Gallup® in any way.

The following authors have been attributed in the creation of this book, and all efforts were made to seek permission to reference appropriately.

- *Good to Great* – Jim Collins
- *Jumpstart Your Marketing Brain* – Doug Hall
- *Strengths-Based Leadership* – Tom Rath
- *Strengths-Based Selling* – Tony Rutigliano & Dr. Brian Brim
- *StrengthsFinder 2.0* – Gallup
- *The Thought Leaders Practice* – Matt Church, Peter Cook, Scott Stein

Editing by Mish Phillips, Lexi Wight and Emily Stephenson
Cover illustration by Cameron Miller
Typesetting and design by David W. Edelstein

ISBN 978-1-922357-56-4 (paperback)
ISBN 978-1-922357-57-1 (ebook)

*To my clients – past, present, and future:
wishing you all an ocean full of FISH, forever.*

CONTENTS

Foreword by Matt Church ix

Acknowledgements xi

Getting Started xiii

Introduction xv

PART I: EARLY UNDERSTANDING   1

Chapter 1
Introduction to FISH 3

Chapter 2
Strengths Philosophy 11

Chapter 3
Business versus Practice 27

Chapter 4
Defining a Strengths-Based Practice 31

PART II: BUILDING FOUNDATIONS   35

Chapter 5
Strengths-Based Purpose 39

Chapter 6
Strengths-Based Values 59

Chapter 7
Strengths-Based Relationships 73

Chapter 8
Strengths-Based Leadership......................... 85

Chapter 9
Strengths-Based Thought Leadership.................. 95

PART III: FINDING RHYTHM   101

Chapter 10
Strengths-Based Marketing 109

Chapter 11
Strengths-Based Selling 117

Chapter 12
Strengths-Based Delivery........................... 129

Chapter 13
Measuring the Practice and FISH 145

PART IV: BRIGHTNESS OF FUTURE   153

Leaving a Legacy 163

Concluding Insights by Lisa O'Neill.................... 167

Work With Me.. 169

About the Author 171

Research Interview Acknowledgements 173

Reader Praise for
Finding FISH in a Strengths-Based Practice 177

Foreword
by Matt Church

It's an honour to write this foreword for Christopher.

Christopher is a kind, gentle, people-centred man. He has survived things one should not need to face. It would be completely reasonable to take a lived experience such as Christopher's and drop into caring only for your kids and surviving day to day. And while Christopher holds no monopoly on tragedy, it is his unwavering commitment to bringing the highest quality of life to the lives of others that makes him remarkable and qualified to write this book. To endure such deep heartache and find a way to be of service to others makes this book and the guidance it contains precious.

As you read this book imagine the author is one of the most attentive, curious and interested people you've met and you will begin to experience not just the intent behind the words but the sentiment that sits behind the motivation to complete this work. The sentiment is that you matter, the work you do matters, and that Christopher is deeply invested in you doing your work and indeed living your life in a way that fills you with fulfilment, inspiration, success and happiness.

I feel a kindred spirit-ness to Christopher in the role he adopts as a coach's coach in this book. To take a moment and not just coach but coach coaches is to multiply one's impact on the planet 100 fold, as each coach goes on to impact the lives of those they serve. I don't think the author of a foreword should talk about themselves or their work too much, if at all, but in this case, it's why I think Christopher asked me to write one. I teach a body of work through the Thought Leaders Curriculum as part of our business school that Christopher references heavily throughout this book. And so my role here as I see it is to endorse Christopher and this book to you and perhaps explain, somewhat, as to why I think he chose to embed so much of what we teach in this book.

I believe that teaching, coaching and inspiring others to be fully self-expressed in service to others is one of the prime deep aspirations towards leadership. Strengths-based coaches do this every day and so lending my hand and imprimatur to this book is a no-brainer.

At Thought Leaders we help experts to figure out how to take their practice out into the world to make a greater impact, and focus this ambition toward the dual goals of meaning and money. We say that we help clever people to be commercially smart doing work they love, with people they like, the way they want. The process Christopher references in this book, something we call The Curriculum, is how we have enabled the success of hundreds perhaps thousands of coaches, speakers, trainers and authors to take their ideas to the world.

At the heart of the philosophy that drives our program is that great thinkers should be free. Indeed, when the world has access to a diverse range of ideas, principles and teachings, it becomes an even better place to live and work. Ideas have the power to change lives, and improving access to these ideas multiplies that impact. Through his work here and in his own thought leader practice, Christopher is encouraging you. Encouraging you as a coach to go next level. He is encouraging you to find your thought leadership and as such greater, fulfilment, inspiration, success, and happiness. And in this, we both agree, that when people turn up fully on the planet and leave nothing behind the world begins to shine a little brighter.

It has been said that all it takes for one person to change their world is for another to believe they can. This is the heart of *encouragement*, the focus of this book and the Tao of Christopher.

Matt Church
Founder, Thought Leaders

Acknowledgements

- To the 21 Practice Owners who commit their time and talent to being the best versions of themselves, and who shared their insights with me in the creation of this book

- To Matt Church, founder of The Thought Leaders Business School and creator of the Pink Sheet – it made this book so much better than my first

- To Lisa O'Neill for her energy, love and support – I am in your debt

- To Col Fink for his ability to disrupt my practice at just the right moments

- To the Thought Leaders and Strengths Communities, without whom this book would not be possible

- To the team at Hambone Publishing – Ben, Mish, Lexi, Emily and David – for believing in the work I do

- To Tash, my extraordinary Practice Manager, for her ability to keep me organised and her contribution to the Strengths-Based Relationships chapter

- To Cameron for his exceptional art work in both of my books so far

- To Ross just for being you

Getting Started

MY FIRST BOOK, *The Joy of Finding FISH,* is an exploration of the FISH principles – Fulfilment, Inspiration, Success, and Happiness. In my personal journey, I discovered that these principles are not absolute truths but rather choices rooted in our state of mind; each of them supports and complements one another without being reliant. They are deeply personal experiences shaped by our purpose, values, sources of inspiration, how we experience and measure success, and what makes us happy in any given moment.

Before you read any further, it might be valuable to pause and consider your own personal definitions of Fulfilment, Inspiration, Success, and Happiness. In *The Joy of Finding FISH,* Chapter 4 lays out a framework for understanding and measuring the elements of FISH:

Fulfilment
FISH Definition: *The experience of living your purpose every single day.*
Ask Yourself: *On a scale of 1 to 10, how much fulfilment did I experience today? How did I live my purpose today?*

Inspiration
FISH Definition: *The spontaneous process of thinking, being, creating, or doing something new and creative.*
Ask Yourself: *On a scale of 1 to 10, how much inspiration did I feel today? What was I inspired to think, create, do, or be today?*

Success

FISH Definition: *The accomplishment of a desirable outcome or experience.*
Ask Yourself: *On a scale of 1 to 10, how successful did I feel today? What were my most outstanding achievements today?*

Happiness

FISH Definition: *Feeling pleasure or being grateful for someone or something.*
Ask Yourself: *On a scale of 1 to 10, how happy did I feel today? What was I most grateful for today? What brought me pleasure?*

While these definitions and questions may seem somewhat arbitrary, they are valuable in determining how to assess and calculate your FISH score.

Having an understanding of these elements, and how they sit for you right now, will be a useful lens to consider as you read the rest of this book.

Introduction

"Every moment is a fresh beginning."

T.S. Eliot

Finding FISH in a Strengths-Based Practice is built enormously on the shoulders of giants. Thought leaders around the world have contributed to the principles built into this book, and the models, stories, and practice theory have been integrated from a number of sources. The following books/authors have been referenced extensively and their theories and intellectual property feature prominently. In each chapter, I have attributed the work of these authors, and wherever appropriate, have sought permission to republish in its current form:

- *Good to Great* by Jim Collins,
- *Jumpstart Your Marketing Brain* by Doug Hall,
- *Strengths-Based Leadership* by Tom Rath,
- *Strengths-Based Selling* by Tony Rutigliano and Brian Brim,
- *StrengthsFinder 2.0* from Gallup,
- *The Joy of Finding FISH: A Journey of Fulfilment, Inspiration, Success, and Happiness* by Christopher Miller,
- *The Thought Leaders Practice* by Matt Church, Peter Cook, and Scott Stein.

I have also had the opportunity to interview 21 owners of Strengths-Based Practices and have learned extensively from their courage and energy in how they run lives and practices to be proud of. I have attempted to use examples and stories from these interviews to demonstrate the many concepts presented in this book. I am so grateful to everyone who took the time to be interviewed; their details can be found in an appendix at the back of this publication.

The hypothesis I set out to explore in writing this book was that when a practice owner plays to their strengths, understands the value of building a practice versus building a business, and surrounds themselves with complementary partners to give themselves the best chance of doing what they love, they have a high likelihood of experiencing fulfilment, inspiration, success, and happiness (FISH) at work and in life. Taken a step further, leading a Strengths-Based Practice becomes a life-choice, rather than a work-choice, and, inspired by Mark Twain, by doing what they love every day, they never have to work another day in their lives. For many, losing the guilt of getting paid to do what you love is part of the journey and goes a long way to redefining what work really is.

This book is divided into four parts:

Part I - Early Understanding: where some of the theories and frameworks are explained in preparation for the later chapters.

Part II - Building Foundations: where the core principles of building a Strengths-Based Practice are explained.

Part III - Finding Rhythm: where the daily, weekly, monthly, and annual priorities of running a Strengths-Based Practice are explored.

Part IV - Brightness of Future: where the inspiration and long-term vision of a Strengths-Based Practice are described.

I am on a mission to help the world experience more fulfilment, inspiration, success, and happiness. For me, running a Strengths-Based Practice is the fastest and easiest way to experience FISH.

I am wishing you, the reader, an ocean full of FISH, whatever passion you might pursue in life and work.

With love,
Christopher

PART I

Early Understanding

> *"The beautiful thing about learning
> is that no one can take it away from you."*
>
> B.B. King

AM JUST so grateful that you have chosen to commit some of your valuable time to exploring this book. *Finding FISH in a Strengths-Based Practice* has been a labour of love for me, combining my passion for Strengths Philosophy, deep belief in FISH (fulfilment, inspiration, success, and happiness), and a commitment to doing what you love and loving what you do. I hope these pages offer some inspiration in expanding FISH and passion in your life by leaning into your natural talents.

CHAPTER 1

Introduction to FISH
(fulfilment, inspiration, success, and happiness)

"The purpose of our lives is to be happy."

Dalai Lama XIV

One of the principles I explored in my first book, *The Joy of Finding FISH*, was that we all have these potential emotions within us, and it is not the pursuit of FISH that is important, but rather the awareness that we are living FISH in every moment of our lives. It is "a journey of fulfilment, inspiration, success, and happiness." When we live life by design – a Thought Leadership principle – we have every opportunity to maximise our FISH experience and discover fulfilment, inspiration, success, and happiness, perhaps in corners we never even expected.

It should be understood that FISH is a very personal journey. The definitions of these, and the way they show up in our lives, are as unique as each person's fingerprint. For the purposes of this book, I have defined FISH as the following:

- **Fulfilment:** the experience of living your purpose every single day.
- **Inspiration:** the spontaneous process of thinking, being, creating, or doing something new and creative.
- **Success:** the accomplishment of a desirable outcome or experience.
- **Happiness:** feeling pleasure or being grateful for someone or something.

As you walk through this book, feel free to use these definitions, or write down definitions that feel more personal and accurate for you.

In the context of running a Strengths-Based Practice, we will later explore:

- The relationship between strengths and purpose/fulfilment.

Which comes first? Which feeds the other? The power of being 'on purpose' and finding your strengths in flow.
- Strengths as a source of inspiration when the practice is running well, or when you are struggling. Finding self-expression in the pursuit and implementation of new ideas, experiences, and energy.
- The significant link between playing to your strengths and generating a track record of achievement over time. Leveraging the right strengths for the desired outcome.
- Finding love and happiness in what you do, knowing you were born to do this, and pausing to appreciate the joy of it all. Feeling grateful for what you have is an amazing source of happiness when you take the time to acknowledge it.

One concept that will be revisited again and again throughout this book is the idea to surround yourself with complementary partners, or those who love doing what you hate, or are very good at tasks and responsibilities that you are terrible at. In order to build a life where you get to **do what you love** most of the time **and get paid for it**, you must find people you trust who are really motivated to do the things that suck the soul out of you. Strengths-Based partnerships ensure that everyone in your practice and your life has the opportunity to experience their FISH by loving what we do, doing what we love, and inspiring those we serve.

In my first book, I introduced a simple measurement system for FISH:

- On a scale of 0-10, how much fulfilment did you experience today? (When were you 'on purpose'?)
- On a scale of 0-10, how much inspiration did you experience today? (What were you inspired by? What were you inspired to do/be?)
- On a scale of 0-10, how successful did you feel today? (And what were your most significant achievements?)

- On a scale of 0-10, how happy did you feel today? (And what were your sources of happiness?)

When I began this journey, I used my FISH score to make a mental note of my best and my worst days. I can name the top and bottom 10 days of my life so far, and how good or bad my FISH score was on those days. Much of this was outlined in *The Joy of Finding FISH*; I made the observation that for most people, a 10:10:10:10 day is a precious unique memory of a perfect day, to be savoured and relished over time. I also stated that 0:0:0:0 days are exceptionally rare, as it is incredibly difficult to rate all four FISH elements at rock bottom. As an example, on the day that my wife died from brain cancer in 2021, my sons and I were all together in the hospice with her when she passed away. While my inspiration, success, and happiness scores were all 0 on that day, my sense of purpose as a father and the need to honour Fiona appropriately as a husband meant that my sense of fulfilment was quite strong that day.

At the time of writing this second book, I have been keeping a daily FISH score in a gratitude journal and now have an eight-month record of my results, along with comments and gratitude statements to capture why my score was the way it was on each given day. I used to give myself an average score for the day – my average sense of fulfilment, average level of inspiration, average feeling of success, and average happiness. But over time, I have found it more useful to record my FISH score based on the best FISH experience each day – when was I **most** on purpose? What was my **most** inspiring moment of the day? What was my **proudest** achievement of the day? When was I the **happiest** throughout the day? The emotion of a single moment can capture the spirit of a day, and the daily challenges are very much put into perspective by acknowledging the meaningful highlights. When faced with the fullness of life's dramas, it is the energy of progress and the feeling it is all worthwhile that keeps us coming back for more.

Finding FISH in a Strengths-Based Practice

7.5-10 Dolphin	Fulfilment	Inspiration	Success	Happiness
	Thriving	Fizzing	Abundant	Ecstatic
5.0-7.5 Koi Fish				
	Fulfilled	Inspired	Successful	Happy
2.5-5.0 Starfish				
	Unfulfilled	Uninspired	Unsuccessful	Unhappy
0-2.5 Clam				
	Lost	Vacant	Failure	Despair

Based on your daily score, you can orient yourself on the table above and identify whether that emotion resonates with you. If not, try to find your own language to describe how you are feeling about your level of fulfilment, inspiration, success, and happiness.

Pause to celebrate any score above an eight (in any category), and seek help from friends, family, or your support network for any scores below a three. I have begun to track FISH scores over time for all of my clients, and the insights are amazing, especially in the integration of professional and personal experiences that contribute to a FISH score.

One of the most valuable questions I often ask a client is 'Which FISH element do you lead with? Which element, when experienced fully, has an automatic flow on effect to the other three? A person who leads with Fulfilment is likely to design their day and their life completely differently to a person who leads with Success. Over time, my clients and I can design actions and behaviours tailored to our FISH preferences, and keeping a score over time allows us to notice if we are shifting the dial on any of the elements.

Thriving, fizzing, abundant, and ecstatic are all potentially desirable emotions or states of being to experience, and it takes practice, lots of self-awareness, and intention to make these a reality. Whilst working with others on their FISH score, I've found it fascinating to see how one person's thriving experience is another's unfulfilled! Our relationship to these emotions is entirely personal, so there is no use in comparing your FISH score to others', as you might be operating on different scales. Some people are unlikely to live life below an eight, which means their FISH scores get most interesting when you compare their 9.1s and 9.3s!

In scoring yourself with FISH, you can focus on how one element feels, or what the average of the four elements appears to be at any one time. To give an extreme example, a 10:10:0:10 score on the surface appears to be okay overall (above 7.5) but the feeling of a lack of success can profoundly erode the other three elements if left unaddressed over time. Identifying your strongest and weakest FISH elements at any given time can provide useful perspective and establish relevant and impactful actions you can take to lift your FISH score.

Similarly, feelings of being lost, vacant, failure, and despair are powerful negative emotions that most of us descend into from time to time. It is important to consider initially how this emotion or state of being is currently serving you. Consider that it might be protective in some way. Then, take the time to explore and reflect on how long you wish to remain in that state. By keeping a FISH score journal, you can usually identify one action or strategy that will pull you out of a low score and into a mid-range or higher score in time. Or a family member, friend, or trusted coach can help you explore options to consider what might brighten the future.

Inspired by the rough scoring system above, I have developed a GoneFISHing diagnostic which can be found on my website (**christopher-miller.com/the-joy-of-finding-fish-diagnostic**). The diagnostic consists of

Finding FISH in a Strengths-Based Practice

83 questions and takes about 20 minutes to complete. The output is a report that offers a score for each FISH element and an overall FISH score, along with a personalised list of recommendations and coaching questions on where to invest time and effort in order to lift the experience of fulfilment, inspiration, success, and happiness at work as well as in life.

In leading a Strengths-Based Practice, you will find activities that have a rich and high FISH score – lean into these and build your reputation behind them. In contrast, you may find activities that suck the life out of you. This is when it becomes important to find a partner, practice manager, virtual assistant, or outsource partner to do anything to get that soul-destroying action off your plate. You could lean in and master that dreaded activity, but you will always resent it and it will draw energy away from what you are best at and what you love to do most!

Sometimes you need to be brave and try something new – you won't be a master at first, but there might be a glimpse of genius coming from you in taking on that activity. My recent experience with public speaking falls under this category. Trepidation, fear, am I good enough, will they listen, will they care (they won't care!) all ran through my mind, but I knew that once I had delivered a successful keynote or presentation, I would have a new way of experiencing FISH, and a new formula for improving my practice reputation and delivery capability.

While I recommend monitoring a FISH score on a daily basis, it can just as easily be tracked weekly, monthly, or annually if you want to take a wider picture of your life. The key is to pick a rhythm and stick to it so that you can gather data over time to compare and contrast. A future development I am committed to is a FISH app, or something similar, that will enable users to keep a personal diary of their FISH score and FISH experiences. If you are interested in being kept up to date with this development, please go to christopher-miller.com.

Linking FISH back to a Strengths-Based Practice, my goal is to demonstrate that if your heart and commitment is to build a life and practice to be proud of, your FISH scores are likely to increase the more you invest in doing what you love and loving what you do.

FISH is a side-effect of running a successful Strengths-Based Practice – you don't pursue FISH, you experience it by getting lost in your purpose, finding inspiration everywhere you look, celebrating achievements, and feeling deeply grateful and happy for everything in your life. At the end of every chapter, I will be asking a few FISH questions to highlight the way strategy, action, and doing are connected to emotion, feeling, and being.

> *As you sit reading this chapter, what is your FISH score right now?*
>
> *What would you like your FISH score to be by the time you finish reading this book?*

CHAPTER 2

Strengths Philosophy

"What will happen when we think about what is right with people rather than fixating on what is wrong with them?"

Don Clifton

I was introduced to Strengths Philosophy in 2010, the year I joined Gallup as Senior Consultant in New Zealand. While I had been a Myers-Briggs and Extended DISC facilitator in the past, and valued these kind of assessment tools, nothing quite prepared me for the impact Strengths had on my life and those of my clients. At its heart, the positive psychology Strengths movement is focused on what is right with people, rather than what is wrong with them. This philosophy is almost more important than the various tools that are available to measure strengths and talent in humanity.

It is probably worth clarifying the definition of a talent versus a strength. StrengthsFinder 2.0, based on the work of Gallup, defines strengths and talents as follows:

1) **Strengths** are the unique combination of talents, knowledge, and skills that every person possesses. They represent the innate abilities that individuals naturally possess and can further develop over time with deliberate practice and refinement. Strengths are the areas where individuals have the greatest potential for growth, excellence, and success.

2) **Talents** are the naturally recurring patterns of thought, feeling, or behavior that can be productively applied. They are the raw materials of strengths and represent the specific ways in which individuals think, feel, and act that enable them to perform at their best. Talents are the building blocks upon which strengths are built, and they provide the foundation for individuals to excel in various areas of their lives.

In summary, strengths are the unique combination of talents, knowledge, and skills that individuals possess and can further develop, while talents are the natural patterns of thought, feeling, or behavior that serve as the foundation for strengths. Understanding and leveraging both strengths and talents can empower individuals to achieve greater levels of success, fulfillment, and well-being in their personal and professional lives.

In the development of my thinking, Strengths preceded my discovery of fulfilment, inspiration, success, and happiness (FISH) as a strategy for measuring a life well-lived. The power of Strengths as a lens to focus on the best version of ourselves led me to explore the outcome, or desired **why** we have for our lives. And while leveraging Strengths to experience fulfilment, inspiration, success, and happiness is a wonderful approach to life, my recent reflections suggest that perhaps there is an even bigger Why – Joy and Love, which are likely to form the core of a future book.

The model on the following page captures the spirit of Evolving Love, and has fundamental implications about the relationship between fulfilment, inspiration, success, happiness, and love.

Time and time again, I have witnessed the impact of Strengths on an individual's self-assurance and confidence in self-expression. Using Strengths as a descriptive vocabulary, I have experienced the awakening of clients and friends from as young as eight years old to those beyond eighty. Clarity of what we do best and what we love most can be a powerful guide to building a future that we can lean into and enjoy, whether it be a person's calling, chosen career or preferred hobbies and pastimes.

FULFILMENT, INSPIRATION...

Evolution of Love

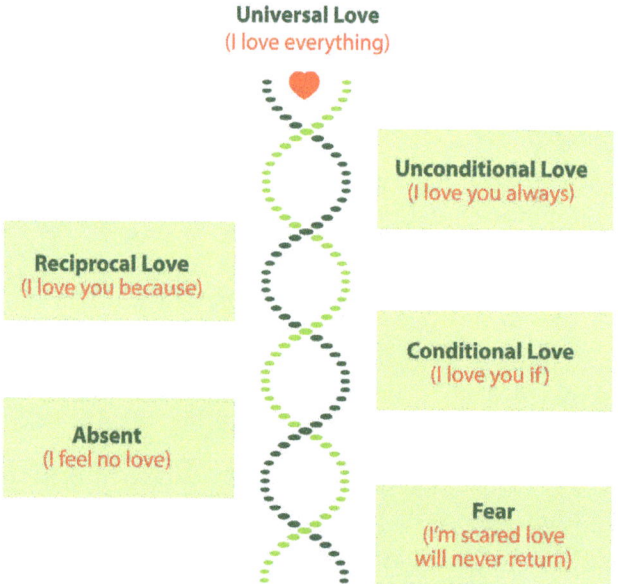

As a result of the inspiration and powerful effectiveness in a Strengths-Based approach, a number of tools have been developed around the world. These can be used to assess your strengths and talents. Each has a slightly different lens or language, but all focus meaningfully on what a person loves to do most, and what they do best in life and work.

Whilst researching for this book, I invested in a number of assessments to compare and contrast their effectiveness and how much meaning or use each brought to me personally. I have summarised the results here, in the order of personal impact on my life over the last 25 years.

STRENGTHS-BASED ASSESSMENTS THAT I'VE USED

Gallup CliftonStrengths (www.gallup.com/cliftonstrengths) – This tool is the one I'm most familiar with tool due to my employment history with Gallup and the extent to which I have witnessed its impact with my clients over a 15-year period. This is my tool of choice for self-awareness, relationship management and personal effectiveness. I have witnessed this tool create fundamental shifts in a person's experience of life. This tool is founded in a huge amount of research over an extended period of time, and has to date over 30 million users worldwide. There is an elegance and very clear intent in mapping humanity to four 'domains' of Strengths, and 34 unique themes.

My dominant themes (definitions are my own rather than Gallup's official definitions):

- Maximiser – constant and never-ending improvement
- Learner – passion for learning and growth
- Connectedness – understanding the connection between all things and all people
- Input – archiving of useful information with intent to retrieve
- Woo – winning others over, persuasion, and influence
- Positivity – optimism, even in the face of adversity
- Activator – starter energy, momentum
- Individualisation – appreciating the uniqueness in others
- Includer – finding reasons to include and being sensitive to exclusion
- Intellection – thoughtful contemplation
- Belief – foundations of core purpose and values
- Self-Assurance – confidence in areas of expertise
- Communication – eloquence in written and spoken word
- Strategic – option-finding; contingency planning
- Relator – connected to an inner circle of trusted friends, colleagues, and family

Myers-Briggs/16 Personalities (www.16personalities.com) – One of the very first self-assessment tools I ever undertook; while it categorises into

16 distinct archetypes, my profile has changed very little over nearly two decades, which reflects the tool's stability and consistency.

My profile is Assertive Protagonist (ENFJ-A):

- Extrovert (rather than Introvert)
- Intuitive (rather than Observant)
- Feeling (rather than Thinking)
- Judging (rather than Prospecting)

Strengths Profile (www.strengthsprofile.com) – A useful complementary tool to CliftonStrengths, containing themes that feel like a combination of talents, strengths, and elements of character. This tool also segments strengths into 'Realised Strengths' (strengths you use and enjoy); 'Unrealised Strengths' (strengths you don't use as often); 'Learned Behaviours' (things you've learned to do but may not enjoy); and 'Weaknesses' (things you find hard and don't enjoy).

- My Realised Strengths are: Mission, Listener, Gratitude, Moral Compass, Unconditionality, Authenticity, and Optimism.
- My Unrealised Strengths are: Compassion, Curiosity, Drive, Resilience, Spotlight, Counterpoint, and Empathic.
- My Learned Behaviours are: Work Ethic, Adventure, Courage, and Improver.
- My Weaknesses are: Competitive, Relationship Deepener, and Humour.

Strengths Deck (www.strengthsdeck.com) – really useful and practical tool that is agnostic to the language of strengths from all the other tools, and offers people a tactile experience in selecting their own strengths profile.

StrengthScope (www.strengthscope.com) – There is lots of validation for this tool and simple conceptually as a 'Significant Seven Strengths.' Themes are chosen from a group of 24 possibilities. Some of the questions are slightly biased toward an employed environment (as opposed to owning a business or practice).

My Significant 7 Strengths:
- Compassion
- Decisiveness
- Developing Others
- Empathy
- Initiative
- Self-Improvement
- Strategic Mindedness

Strengths-Based Resilience (based on VIA – www.strengthsbased-resilience.com) – Signature Strength Questionnaire (SSQ-72) – A useful free alternative to Strengths Profile and offers a similar combined view of character and strengths.

My top strengths are:
- Gratitude
- Honesty, Integrity, Authenticity and Genuineness
- Persistence, Industry, Diligence and Perseverance
- Creativity and Originality
- Hope, Optimism and Future-Mindedness.

StandOut Assessment (www.standout.tmbc.com) – An interesting assessment with a largely 'employee' perspective (as opposed to business owner or practice owner). This tool offers nine distinct archetypes that characterise your dominant strengths.

My top two roles were Connector and Pioneer.

Red Bull Wingfinder (www.redbull.com/int-en/wingfinder) – The most unique questionnaire combining visual preferences, problem solving, and pattern recognition. I found this the most challenging to draw conclusions between the survey and the results.

Creativity
- Classical rather than open to experience
- Innovative rather than pragmatic
- Adaptable rather than focused

Drive
- Slightly more achiever than patient
- Slightly more relaxed than disciplined
- Slightly more modest than confident

Thinking
- A balanced learner (not agile or intuitive)

Connections
- Autonomous rather than supportive
- Direct not diplomatic
- Slightly more balanced than emotive
- Slightly more independent than sociable

USEFUL INSIGHTS FROM THESE STRENGTHS-BASED ASSESSMENTS

From my own results, here are a few insights to consider:

- Every tool offers a different perspective about your strengths, talents, or character traits.

Finding FISH in a Strengths-Based Practice

- Each tool is only as good as your input. There is no point in answering the questions the way you wish to be perceived, or the way you think others perceive you, but rather focus on honest reflection of your own behaviours and preferences.
- Each tool has a different level of research and validity behind it, but the results can be no less insightful if you answer the assessment honestly.
- There is more variety than I expected across the various tools, but the results are largely congruent and complementary.
- Each tool has a different level of robustness behind it, backed by research and evidence over time; each also has a different user cost - many of the tools with the highest level of investment create the most impactful personal insights (you get what you pay for?)
- While insight from multiple tools is beneficial, there is a law of diminishing returns in that there are fewer lightbulb moments as you undertake more tools.
- Most of the tools seek to identify behaviour and strengths in five key areas and rely on **preference**, **frequency** and **aptitude** to determine:
  - How do you CREATE something new?
  - How do you GET STUFF DONE?
  - How do you INSPIRE yourself or others?
  - How do you CONNECT to the world around you?
  - How do you THINK?

The following sites offer a useful review of a variety of available strengths tools that all serve a slightly different purpose.

- www.positivepsychology.com/strength-finding-tests
- www.myleadershipstrengths.com/blog/best-strengths-assessment-tools

Daria Williamson is an author I admire in this space who has done a robust analysis of three of the most popular tools – CliftonStrengths, VIA, and Strengths Profile. Interestingly, each of these tools has unearthed strength themes that overlap and are common between them, yet each also has brought to light strengths in humanity that appear to be unique to each tool. So if you want to uncover the strength of Humility, you would need to do Strengths Profile, or discovering Connectedness would require you to undertake CliftonStrengths, but you are likely to discover Achiever, Drive, and Work Ethic whichever tool you choose. Daria has gone a step further and developed a set of Strength Deck cards that leverage the best content across several tools and serve as a tactile tool to identifying what your strengths pattern might be. Her book, *Unleash Your Awesome,* and her Strengths Deck cards can be ordered from www.strengthsdeck.com.

My 'Zone of Genius' using The Strengths Deck included: Amplifier, Courageous, Grateful, Legacy, Lifelong Learner, Listener, Purposeful, Personaliser, Hopeful, and Self-Aware. The Strengths Deck also helped uncover my areas of potential, reputation, proficiency, and zone of indifference. It is a self-select methodology but offers a deep and rich variety of strengths to choose from and clear instructions of how best to use The Strengths Deck.

IN CONCLUSION

My own feeling is that strength themes are like wisdom in that they represent 'truth that lifts humanity'. Building a Strengths-Based approach has the potential to enhance any relationship: with yourself, in your family, at work, and in life generally. It is perhaps unimportant which tool you choose to identify your strengths; the power is in growing your self-awareness and your conviction in living your strengths fully every single day.

Finding FISH in a Strengths-Based Practice

Strengths themes are inherently positive in nature, though some rich insights can be gained by exploring when a strength might be over-expressed, or strengths that are not your preference and therefore a relative weakness. Before proceeding with this book, there might be value in investing in your own Strengths assessment (choose the one that feels right for you) which would bring many of this book's models and examples to life. If you don't do an assessment the first time around, the book might bear reading again once you have completed a strengths assessment.

One quick way to consider your strengths would be to complete the following Love Most Matrix, which is based upon many of the principles of strengths philosophy, and simplifies the intention of many of the tools outlined above.

In work and in life, consider:

* What activities and responsibilities do you love most?
* Which ones do you love least?
* What activities and responsibilities do you do best?
* Which do you 'do worst'?

Love Most	Love Least
What do I love most at work and in life?	What do I love least at work and in life?
Do Best	Do Worst
What do I do best, better than 90% of those around me?	What do I dread doing, because I am so bad at it or it causes me so much stress?

Your love most/do best items will likely give you an indication of your strengths and/or natural talents, while your love least/do worst items are areas where you should explore delegating or finding a complementary partner who can take on those tasks.

Strengths philosophy is perhaps more powerful than any tool in itself, as it shapes our attitude and psychology in the way we view the world around us. Imagine supporting and celebrating an academic subject where your child was achieving an A grade; helping them to take their learning to a new, even higher level of understanding and, more importantly, enjoyment. Why wrap around support like tutoring and extra time invested in a subject they find difficult and/or unenjoyable? The same choices take place in our workplaces every day.

Strengths is not a stand-alone concept. It is important to understand where to apply or aim your strengths. You will notice that this book does not treat strengths as an isolated entity, but rather as a catalyst for achieving specific outcomes (e.g. Strengths-Based purpose, Strengths-Based marketing). Wherever possible, I have used examples of Strengths-Based Practice owners I have interviewed for this book, or I have used myself as a case study. Strengths will give you an opportunity to hypothesise about what activities in a Strengths-Based Practice you will enjoy the most or be exceptional at. It may also offer suggestions about how to tackle a task you usually don't enjoy, by leveraging your talent in other areas, or choosing to surround yourself with other preferences (think putting good music on and enjoying a glass of wine before tackling bookkeeping, if you haven't already delegated that task!).

My Maximiser (#1) and Input (#4) themes (CliftonStrengths) have a certain intuition about combining other people's intellectual property to hopefully create something useful and insightful for others. You will see examples of this throughout the book such as:

- Combining The Four Needs of Followers (*Strengths-Based Leadership* – Tom Rath) with Four Elements of Great Companies (*Good to Great*, Jim Collins) to create a Strengths-Based Leadership Matrix.
- Combining Doug Hall's three elements of great marketing (*Jumpstart Your Marketing Brain*) with the four domains of CliftonStrengths to create Strengths-Based Marketing actions.

Finding FISH in a Strengths-Based Practice

Most of the language I use to describe the various models in the book have come from my 15 years of coaching and mentoring people using Strengths language and philosophy through my own lens, but I am aware that my choice of language may have a bias based on how I perceive each theme and how it expresses itself. Everyone is unique, and I am still learning every day about other people's perception and acknowledgement of their own themes. Especially for other experienced Strengths coaches who read this book, please take my interpretation with a grain of salt and substitute with your own insights and learnings where appropriate. Given my need to archive useful information and appeal to a wide audience, I would value feedback on how the flow and content of this book resonates with the Strengths tool that most resonates with you.

There is always more than one way of doing things. If you feel your leading or strongest themes are all similar or predictable in defining the approach you might take with a problem, dig deeper down your profile and explore how themes further down your list, or themes from more than one tool help explore the variety of possible paths to finding a solution. Alternatively, consider taking a new and different profiling tool to unearth a new language to describe your strengths. If you are able to identify a meaningful deficit (something in your lower themes) it may be time to go on a search for a complementary partner who can compensate for your weakness. There is very little value in investing in a theme in the lower half of your profile because, at best, it will become an 'average' talent of yours. Your superpower lies among your dominant themes at the top of your profile, which, when invested in, become talents that light you up and define your reputation as well as your impact on the world. When you invest in your strongest themes, you get a much greater return on investment, and have a higher likelihood of:

- CREATING something new
- INSPIRING yourself or others

- CONNECTING to the world around you
- GETTING STUFF DONE
- Developing new and unique THOUGHTS.

Taken a step further, the positioning and reputation of your Strengths-Based Practice may be informed or even built upon the foundations of your dominant themes. Your purpose, values, internal and external relationships, the way you market and sell your practice, your choice of delivery methods, leadership style, and your pursuit of a Greatest Imaginable Challenge (a concept I explore in my first book) may all be determined by how you leverage your top talents, and where you experience the greatest enjoyment and impact.

Wouldn't it be wonderful if we could all play to our strengths every day? What if work felt more like play all the time? How would 'work' feel like if there was more joy and less effort? Rather than focus on fixing a weakness, how much more effective would it be to overwhelm a weakness with a strength? For example, your ability to inspire and lead others might be the catalyst to surround yourself with a whole team of talented workhorses who get stuff done on your behalf (and they love doing it because it plays to their strengths!). In a typical Strengths journey, an individual moves from a lack of awareness about where their talent lies, to an emerging awareness about what they are good at, to practising and refining their genius, and then, finally, towards developing mastery. In mastery, playing to your strengths feels so natural that nothing really feels like work again.

Finding FISH in a Strengths-Based Practice

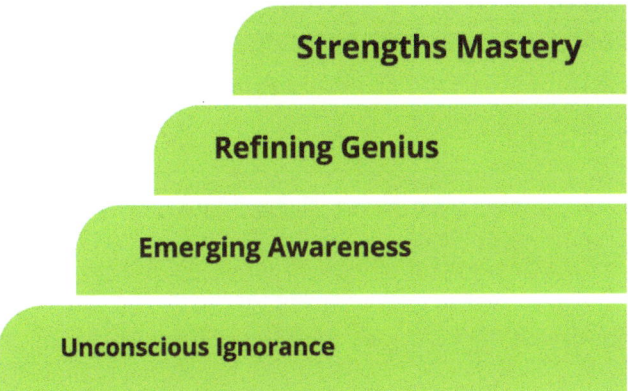

At its heart, Strengths philosophy encourages people to love what they do every day, and it is often helpful to map out what you love most in life and at work, **and** what you love least. Your love least may be someone else's love most – the trick is to find that someone and create a complementary partnership. Doing what you love most and playing in your passion creates an irony of guilt that may require unlearning, especially if you get paid to do what you love most. Your value to those around you is exponential when you invest in what you love to do. Loving what you do and doing what you love creates a passion and authenticity that lifts effectiveness and impact with the world around you.

Similar to doing what you love, doing what you do best creates an upward spiral of performance that you can build on day after day. Knowing and getting feedback about what you do best (and what you do worst) can be a useful investment that lifts self-awareness and helps identify where your greatest effectiveness lies. It takes courage to know in your heart which of your talents are 95 percent stronger than everyone you know. It takes deep humility to truly believe in your own talent. Our uniqueness in the world is captured by many of the tools described in this chapter, and the chances that you share your exact profile with another human being are ridiculously low. We are all designed to make powerful and unique contributions to the world, beginning with our families and those we hold dear. It is our responsibility to keep developing into the best version of ourselves, and investing in our strengths is one of the most impactful ways to add value and experience fulfilment, inspiration, success, and happiness.

> *How might your FISH score be influenced by whether you bring a Strengths-Based lens to your practice?*
>
> *Which of your natural talents or strengths has the greatest impact on your FISH score today?*

> *"Because we're all different people*
> *we occupy complex roles with different experiences,*
> *and we have different dominant themes and strengths.*
> *It's about finding what works best for you as a person."*
>
> Murray

CHAPTER 3

Business versus Practice

"Your work is going to fill a large part of your life, and the only way to be truly satisfied is to do what you believe is great work."

Steve Jobs

IN SEPTEMBER 2017, when I left management consulting to set up my own coaching and mentoring services, I was under the illusion that I was setting up a business – profit and loss, administration, office, infrastructure – with a long-term goal of training other coaches.

Thankfully in 2019, a generous guy called Peter Cook gifted me a copy of *The Thought Leaders Practice,* an extraordinary book by Matt Church, Peter Cook, and Scott Stein. One of the earliest chapters in *The Thought Leaders Practice* is a detailed explanation of the differences between a business and a practice. Typically, there is a perception that a fulfilling career either involves getting a job and working for someone else or starting/buying a business and having other people work for you. *The Thought Leaders Practice* showed me that there is another way: to run a practice rather than a business.

With the blessing of the extraordinary Matt Church, co-founder of Thought Leaders Business School, I have summarised the chapter about business versus practice and added my insights about being a Strengths-Based Practice.

Often, a business is characterised by a lot of assets, requiring many people for operations or delivery, a physical office (usually), management structure and decision making, with low cashflow and low margins. The goal of running a business is to (eventually) have it operate without the owner being involved in the day-to-day rhythm. The exit strategy for a business owner is either sale, successor, or die in the saddle.

In contrast, a practice is characterised by low assets, maximum one or two employees supporting the practice owner, a home office (usually), high cashflow and high margins, and decisions resting with the practice owner and their small, trusted team. One of the key features of a practice is that it is entirely dependent on the skills, talent, and energy of the practice owner for the life of the practice. The practice owner's reputation and essence are intrinsically linked to the success of the practice. The objectives of the practice owner are largely informed by how they prioritise and define fulfilment, inspiration, success, and happiness (FISH).

This distinction offers a link back to Strengths philosophy, where the unique way that the practice owner and their team express themselves and add value to the world form the core of the strategy and direction of the practice. A highly efficient and responsive practice team become known for that productivity, which enhances the reputation of the practice. A practice owner who is good at inspiring others becomes known for their ability to lead from the stage and wow an audience. The intention of this book is to help practice owners clarify and own their natural talent and leadership style to become more impactful.

While businesses can deliver both products and services, a practice is usually dominated by service delivery models, though there are exceptions to the rule. In my interviews of 20 SB Practices, all but one featured service delivery as the main source of income, and the one involving product could be described as a highly consultative, trust-driven relationship with clients that relied heavily on the reputation and authenticity of the practice owner (James Blackie, The Art Counsel).

Within this book, I predominantly refer to the characteristics of a Strengths-Based Practice, with specific reference throughout to the benefit of leveraging a Strengths profile or the Love Most Matrix to inform the talent, energy, and skillset of the practice owner.

Some of the constructs of Thought Leadership, as advocated by Matt Church, Peter Cook, and Scott Stein, are referred to later in the book where relevant and helpful, and I have offered a perspective that intentionally builds a Strengths lens into these concepts.

> *Based on the definitions above, are your strengths more suited to a business or a practice?*
>
> *Which vehicle (job, business, or practice) will lift your fulfilment, inspiration, success, and happiness the most?*

CHAPTER 4

Defining a Strengths-Based Practice

"The road to success is dotted with many tempting parking spaces."

Will Rogers

Strengths philosophy would suggest that doing what you love, and what you are naturally and exceptionally good at, are the keys to sustainable high-performance in life. In this book, we explore the implications of this when leading a Strengths-Based Practice, but the same is true for a career or running a business.

A Strengths-Based Practice consists of a practice owner with one or two support staff, and is reliant on the individual and collective talents of this team to add exceptional value and energy to the people they serve. A Strengths-Based Practice is a labour of love, where all members of the practice team are able to play to their diverse strengths every day, and are surrounded by opportunities for fulfilment, inspiration, success, and happiness (FISH). Some of the prevalent emotions coming from my own Strengths-Based Practice are that we love what we do, do what we love, and inspire those we serve.

In order to maximise success and build a reputation on solid foundations, the practice owner especially must continuously work on self-awareness and self-management, exploring what they love most, knowing what they love least, developing what they do best into a superpower, and delegating or outsourcing what they do worst. Over time, the practice's services and positioning will be intentionally designed around the talents of the practice team, making it easier to run and naturally more successful.

Investing in talent at the right time may also be critical to the success of the practice. Having the courage to position into a new market, try a new form of delivery, or be brave with a new message may all be made easier or more successful if these decisions are backed by the right choice of strengths or combination of strengths (Based in Thought Leaders principles). Surrounding yourself with advisors, coaches, or mentors who have walked your path before **and** are willing to understand and honour your unique Strengths formula will be key to unlocking your success.

Finding FISH in a Strengths-Based Practice

The journey from starting a new Strengths-Based Practice to a mature practice 10 years later is characterised by the repetitive use of a strength to create consistently high performance – it gets easier and better over time, kind of like building a muscle at the gym.

Tracking progress may come in the form of flow experiences – almost magical moments of genius, ease, and connection to a task, relationship, or activity. These flow experiences can offer a roadmap toward success and fulfilment. Once such experiences have been found, it is worth investing in a formula to repeat them, knowing that venturing out and trying new things may be the key to the next flow experience. Perhaps the journey toward mastery is the ease with which we can access flow experiences, knowing that repetition and hard work may be required to reach that state of magic.

Given that a well-run Strengths-Based Practice, over time, will involve up to three talented individuals working together, complementary partnerships are an essential ingredient to optimise. As previously identified, Strengths tools have an uncanny resemblance to each other, with significant overlap in themes as well as a number of unique strengths that are only obvious from undertaking a specific assessment. Regardless of which Strengths language you choose, one of the exercises I enjoy sharing with my clients is a complementary conversation between any two people where we explore:

- How do our strength themes complement each other?
- Why is our partnership 'fit for purpose'?
- How do my strengths off-set your weaknesses and vice versa?
- What can we do together that we cannot do separately?

In the early stages of a Strengths-Based Practice, the owner may be operating on their own. The concept of complementary partnerships is no less important when considering outsource partners who may lift the reputation of the practice. Your choice of bookkeeper, accountant, graphic designer, print supplier, or serviced office all need to fill strengths and talent capability that you do not or cannot on your own. We will discuss later in the book the importance of value and purpose fit for any internal or external complementary partners.

Playing to your strengths involves engaging a unique combination of loving what you do and feeling confident and good about your capability. It creates the paradox that what comes easy (what doesn't feel like work) is usually where you add the most value. Feeling comfortable with getting paid to do what you love means you will never work another day in your life. For those who have optimised running a Strengths-Based Practice, this is exactly what life feels like.

> *Which of your strengths contribute most to your sense of fulfilment, inspiration, success, and happiness?*
>
> *For you, what is the most exciting aspect of running a Strengths-Based Practice?*

PART II

Building Foundations

"I have failed again and again throughout my life. That is why I succeed."

Michael Jordan

Before launching a Strengths-Based Practice in earnest, there are some fundamentals to reflect on. These will become the solid foundations that will serve you as the practice owner, the team that surrounds you, and the clients you serve.

First among these foundations is developing a Strengths-Based **integrated purpose**. Given the fact that a practice relies on the reputation and identity of the practice owner, it is valuable to clarify your personal purpose as the owner, the practice purpose, and – where possible and relevant – simplify these into an integrated purpose. Your strengths profile may also inform either the purpose itself or how the purpose is likely to be lived and experienced at the highest level. Exploring your team members' core senses of purpose may also pay dividends in ensuring that practice purpose is congruent and aligned to the collective purposes of everyone contributing to the practice's success.

Similarly, a set of Strengths-Based **integrated values** can help guide the principles of the practice and will likely benefit from understanding the core values of everyone in the practice team. Given that we all bring our whole selves to work, it is critical to integrate our core life values along with our core work values in articulating the integrated values at play with all members of the practice team. The team's dominant strengths may define core values, or they may help identify how these values are likely to show up in the day-to-day running of the practice.

While relatively small, a Strengths-Based Practice relies heavily on the quality of relationships within the team, and trust is often built on shared experience and mutual respect for the unique talents each person brings to the organisation. Mapping the **complementary Strengths partnerships** across the team is a vital step in ensuring everyone is positioned to do what they love and what they do best, while delegating or outsourcing what they love least and what they do worst. It is essential to consciously identify why a complementary partnership is thriving and invest in strategies to lift the effectiveness of that partnership even further.

The practice owner's **leadership style** has a role to play in how they lead their team, and how they bring leadership to their strategic partners, their outsource partners, and their clients. Conscious competence around how their dominant themes contribute to their leadership style will ensure a level of authenticity and effectiveness in all their key relationships. Understanding whether they lead with Purpose, Values, Brand, or Vision (inspired by Jim Collins' *Good to Great*) and whether they are most suited to inspiring Hope, Trust, Stability, or Compassion (inspired by Tom Rath's *Strengths-Based Leadership*) can help simplify a practice owner's focus when leading others.

A complementary example of a Strengths-Based Practice is those running a Thought Leadership Practice (see book of the same name by Matt Church, Peter Cook, and Scott Stein). One of the principles of being a Thought Leader is the discipline to focus on thinking, selling, and delivering in the service of others through your unique contribution to the world. The Thought Leaders journey involves climbing a belt ladder (like the martial arts) which stipulates specific actions at each stage of the ladder. I offer a Strengths-Based lens to the Thought Leaders journey, and suggest choosing actions to support thinking, selling, and delivery that are congruent with the dominant strength themes of the practice owner. This has the potential to make the journey more effective, faster, and more enjoyable along the way.

These fundamentals are outlined in the next section of the book, prior to discussing how best to run a Strengths-Based Practice (Part III) and how to plan for the long term (Part IV).

> *How will the fundamentals outlined above contribute to your experience of FISH in building and leading a Strengths-Based Practice?*
>
> *Which of your significant strengths will be most useful in exploring the foundations of your practice?*

CHAPTER 5

Strengths-Based Purpose

"I only discovered my life purpose when I discovered Clifton Strengths. Throughout my career, I mostly loved what I did, and I believe I did it well. Without knowing it, I was playing to my top Strengths most of the time, but it was unlocking my Strengths and the language of Strengths that has been life-changing for me – and I want every person I meet to experience the same! I never thought of coaching, but instead coaching and Strengths found me, and here I am, living out my purpose."

Bev Shipley, Chief Inspiration Officer, Open 2 Growth

FULFILMENT, INSPIRATION...

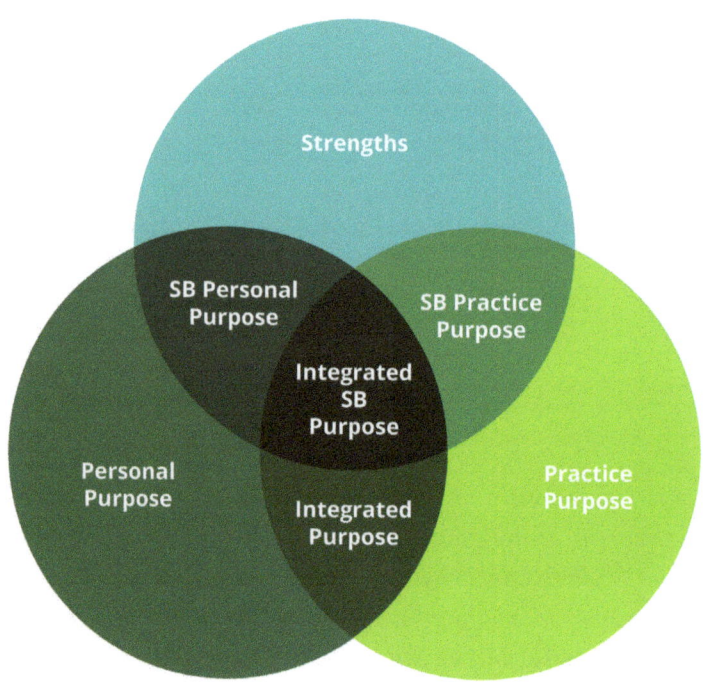

A TREE OFFERS SHADE, provides a home for birds, absorbs carbon dioxide and produces oxygen – these are a few of its many valuable purposes. Perhaps **sustaining life** is a tree's integrated purpose.

I am struck by the fact that human beings are the only living species on the planet with the privilege of being able to choose and voice our unique purpose every single day. Purpose is a very personal topic, and one that I was reluctant to coach in my first few years as a qualified coach. Somehow exploring purpose with a client feels close to the soul, and not to be taken lightly. With experience, I have realised that we can treat purpose more lightly, as an experiment in our lives to give us direction and meaning. You might choose to define your purpose for a day, a week, a month, a year, or even a lifetime.

Integrating purpose offers powerful clarity for living a life well-lived.

It ensures that we are able to live a life congruently, and removes friction from the dynamics of life and work/practice. Given that we all play a huge number of life roles, an integrated purpose also simplifies our ability to fulfil these roles, and helps us bring the best version of ourselves to every situation.

After several months or years running a Strengths-Based Practice, it is clear that the owner's personal or life's purpose becomes inseparable from the practice's purpose. Without even trying, these purposes begin to weave together and either become so congruent as to be seamless, or a whole lot of conflict goes on in the life and practice of the owner because these foundational elements are incongruent or in direct opposition to one another.

This integrated purpose is kind of like all the parts of a tree – roots, trunk, branches, leaves – which all serve a different purpose in the life of the tree, and all provide a different function to the deeper purpose of sustaining life. Roots absorb nutrients and are in symbiosis with the earth; the trunk provides structure and height so that the tree can thrive; branches provide reach and a home for birds; leaves serve to exchange carbon dioxide for oxygen – all of which contribute to the welfare of the planet. Like a tree, the higher purpose of a practice and the practice owner may not be obvious or even apparent, but the power is in providing direction and firm foundations to build upon.

Integrated purpose is the overarching purpose made up of all the separate sub-purposes of your life. Over time, you may ebb and flow through many purposeful moments, and find many definitions of how you choose to express your purpose during any given situation. Your integrated purpose is the sum total of all of these connections to purpose. At any given time, you may have a primary integrated purpose that represents how you engage with the world at a specific point in time, but it is useful to treat this lightly and allow clarity of purpose to emerge spontaneously, as that might redefine your integrated purpose in order to serve you more fully. Ideally, your integrated purpose feels congruent, symbiotic and connected. It is not essential to live all elements of your purpose simultaneously, just know that each version of your purpose over time has served you in a specific circumstance.

As an example of this, I have lived and captured my integrated purpose statement over many years, and I go back to 'old' purpose statements that I have forgotten or bring out of retirement to serve me in the present moment:

- To be a great dad, loving husband, an extraordinary coach and help my clients thrive in life and business.
- To honour Fiona in everything I do. To unconditionally love and support our boys to thrive. To live FISH fully and raise FISH in the world.
- To make dreams come true.
- To help people with passion realise their potential.
- To survive the unthinkable.
- To experience love in all its forms.

A Strengths-Based Purpose is one that acknowledges and leverages your natural talent to shape your purpose. Various Strengths tools offer language that is relevant to character or behaviour, or define a category of natural talent. These can all be built upon to either elicit your integrated purpose or how you go about living this purpose every single day. In my examples above, 'To live FISH fully and raise FISH in the world' is a direct reflection of my #1 CliftonStrengths theme, Maximiser, while 'To make dreams come true' is more closely associated with my #3 theme, Connectedness. My Belief theme makes me somewhat obsessed with the topics of values and purpose, and I have to adapt my coaching style when my client has Belief much lower in their sequence.

The model that opens this chapter suggests that a good starting point to articulate purpose would be to:

Finding FISH in a Strengths-Based Practice

- List your dominant Strengths themes, and which of these is most relevant to discovering your personal or practice purpose.
- Consider what your personal or life purpose is.
- Consider what the purpose of your practice is.
- How do your strengths contribute to each of your personal and practice purpose?
- Where do personal and practice purpose overlap, or where is their greatest congruence?

Purpose can be explored in a number of different ways, but my favourite is to stimulate possibility through powerful questions. The following table offers an approach to expanding from personal or practice purpose to an integrated purpose.

Personal Purpose	Integrated Purpose	Practice Purpose
What is my purpose?	How are my personal and practice purposes complementary?	What is the purpose of my practice?
What am I here to contribute?	How is my practice a vehicle for maximising my contribution to the world?	How can I contribute most to my chosen markets?
Why am I here?	What is the bigger/higher reason for leading a practice at this time?	Why does my practice exist?
What problem am I here to solve?	What problem am I uniquely poised to solve as practice owner?	What problem(s) does my practice solve?
What 'dent' do I want to leave in the universe?	Why is leading a practice at this time more likely to create a 'dent' in the universe? (Steve Jobs)	What 'dent' can my practice make in the universe?
What would I like my legacy to be?	How will my legacy be shaped by fully expressing myself through leading a practice?	What legacy can I create through my practice?

The Strengths-Based Practice owners I interviewed all had a deep connection to purpose. Many were intimately familiar with CliftonStrengths; some had used the tool sporadically, and one interviewee was also engaged in Thought Leadership.

What was fascinating was the variety and mix of purpose statements that fell into one of three categories: **1) Stand-alone purpose statement, 2) Purpose statement informed or influenced by the practice owner's core strengths, and 3) Strengths being the core of the practice owner's purpose.**

Integrated Purpose Statements:

"How can I be a catalyst to ignite potential in others so they can make more of a positive impact in our world?" – **Antonia**

"Offer something that is cutting edge and science-based and helpful to as many people as we can impact." – **Michelle**

"With intent, as much intention as being purposeful would command, and that's like being a good mum, a good and loving nana, a loving partner. Those are expectations that I have of myself, rightly or wrongly. Sometimes, it can take away from the purposefulness of those engagements." – **Lyncia**

"My core purpose is to see people grow, to see them. My tagline for a long time has been 'better tomorrow than you are today'. I like to learn from learners." – **Holly**

"I will do my absolute best to partner with other people to ensure that whatever we do, we get done." – **Charlotte**

"To help organisations do amazing things on the world stage. My business aims to help organisations strengthen the commercial relationships to help improve the procurement experience for people, whether as a supplier or as an internal customer of procurement. One of those things is the belief that New Zealand can do so much and that we can do amazing things on the world stage. And that does help to find my purpose. My desire to see New Zealand thrive is unwavering." – **Sarah**

"I exist to support, encourage and inspire people to live more meaningful lives."
– **Jennifer**

"I get an awful lot of fulfilment from the relationships that I have." – **Lyncia**

"My purpose is helping other people and Strengths is a way to help do that for me."
– **Charlotte**

"First, learn to look for the things in your life that are fabulous, and those that aren't, and then do something about them. It's time for some of those to move on. There might be relationships or your grandmother's old china plate that you never liked. It could be something as simple as that. Start building your life from a platform of 'everything I have here around me is stuff that I want, that I treasure, that I'm in some way connected to'." – **Lyncia**

"It's about creating a legacy and how you want to be remembered in the world." – **Joe**

"Helping others grow and generating an income to support my family's needs."
– **Holly**

"My purpose in business is about building capacity. And that capacity is in individuals, teams, organisations and the community." – **Nicole**

Finding FISH in a Strengths-Based Practice

"Feeling understood and accepted has been pivotal in my own life, shaping my purpose. This personal need drives me to create understanding and help others feel understood in both my personal life and professional practice. My purpose is about building bridges between people, making space for open dialogue and mutual understanding." – **Marina**

"I was called to coach as part of my way of being and purpose. And then, when I discovered Clifton Strengths, it was like, a validation and an encouragement and added to that approach." – **Murray**

"I see my purpose and work purpose being very closely aligned, which also plays into my spiritual purpose—what I want to offer the world, and what I want to bring to the world. It's about helping organisations. I work with senior leadership teams, helping them create cultures that bring out the best in people, so they flourish in their home life. They do not have to sacrifice one or the other." – **Teri**

"I want to create ripples in the world through the work I do with coaching and training." – **Michelle**

"I'm motivated by potential, by eliminating waste. My purpose in life is not to waste." – **Lyncia**

"I've got three to do with helping others in my top five. I worked in bars and restaurants when I was younger, and was terrible. My friend was working in a residential home and helping the elderly, so then I started with that, and I just loved it. From such a young age, I was like, 'There's something about helping others'. That really energises me, motivates me." – **Vicki**

FULFILMENT, INSPIRATION...

Purpose Statements Informed by Strengths:

*"My purpose statement is my 'why',
my strengths help me with the 'how'."*
– Antonia

"From a Strategic perspective, I can read the professional aspects and opportunities and then meet people where they're at. My Relator and my Individualisation help me connect with my clients. And then my Activator has been described by many people. It's just contagious energy." **– Caren**

"I start with delivering. I love that that's the piece that I enjoy. If I could be in front of a group in a room every day, I'd be in my element. If I've got a group of introverted, intelligent learner deliberative, I will use my Individualisation to understand their wants better."
– Charlotte

"You're trying to dig deep here, especially in the coaching arena, developing that relationship, being able for them to feel comfortable to share—that helps drive that Development piece." **– Holly**

"I can inspire someone and aim to help them in a hour, though I enjoy supporting them over time even more. So that's my Relator for sure. I'm also a Maximizer. I see the strengths in people and want to make the most of them. And I have high Positivity and Communication. So I love to help people communicate their value and express their strengths. So I feel like encouraging people uses all of my strengths together." **– Jennifer**

SUCCESS AND HAPPINESS...

Finding FISH in a Strengths-Based Practice

"As a person of faith, one of my core values is loving God and loving people. High relationship-building Empathy is number one. I care about people; I want to help people." – **Holly**

"I think that Achiever, Significance, and Learner are the three strengths that I really lean on in terms of living my purpose. I like to Achieve, I like to hit goals, but I also like to do it in a way that's meaningful and that has an impact. And I like to learn along the way." – **Joe**

"The Maximiser and Relator thing is coming together. How can the most be made out of these relationships, and how can this important relationship be made even better? How do they impact my strategic planning or view? In a coaching context I am often thinking of how a person might be positively impacted by a relationship with someone I know. I believe that there is always a better way and that better way can often be achieved with the help of others" – **Lyncia**

"Individualisation, I guess that helps me from a service perspective to think about what my clients think. I could try and put myself in their shoes and understand what they're trying to achieve." – **Sarah**

"It's deep, authentic relationships with others. Then if I think about the purpose of me and the purpose of my practice, it is about how I can create that space for people to learn to grow to be their best selves, and to achieve what they want to achieve through being their best selves." – **Murray**

IN A LIFE WELL-LIVED

"It's just lovely to get such a variety of relationships; people's relationship to purpose, values and strengths is quite different and unique. Our acceptance and our appreciation of those differences—different mindsets, different emotional states—makes the world a richer place." – **Murray**

"I feel driven to share what I know with people. It allows me to see how I can connect with others. I often introduce people to other people or to resources that I think could be useful for them. Part of my purpose in building capacity is a spirit of generosity." – **Nicole**

"A part of my purpose is to help people through building communities. And just understanding these are the things that energise me and make me enjoy my well-being that day and that sense of purpose." – **Vicki**

"My purpose is deeply grounded in my relationship-building strengths. Individualization and Empathy allow me to understand people intuitively. Connectedness helps me build bridges, fostering meaningful conversations and relationships. My Developer strength drives me to not only observe and connect but also actively support others in their personal growth, helping them be at their best." – **Marina**

"It's having a kind of intuitive gift for other people's strengths. I need to help other people discover their gifts because the world needs what they have to offer. If we don't, if we don't uncover that, we're missing out on a tremendous amount of potential for other people." – **Ty**

Finding FISH in a Strengths-Based Practice

Strengths Becoming the Purpose:

"What I want my clients to be able to feel is what I felt when I first took the Strengths Assessment. I want to give other people the ability to believe in a strengths-based approach, because it then allows them to silence the voices in their head that are telling them they're not good enough." – **Anne**

"My purpose from a professional solopreneur entrepreneur perspective is to introduce individuals to their strengths and then help them think about how to embed them every day in all they do." – **Caren**

"I want to be known for my work on practical strengths. I want to be known for teaching strengths as a second language. So I'm focused on bringing those to life." – **Jo**

"Fortunately, my whole purpose is based on my Strengths profile and how I discovered my purpose."
– **Antonia**

"As long as I'm living in my strengths and ability to express myself through my strengths, I'm very content and very satisfied." – **Jo**

IN A LIFE WELL-LIVED   51

FULFILMENT, INSPIRATION...

"Being able to use my strengths to help people, to help them see themselves in a different light, to help them see the world in a different way, that's what brings me the most joy." – **Jo**

"By understanding those strengths, I support individuals in developing personal strategies that result in team excellence." – **Caren**

"I realised the thing that I loved most was supporting people in my team to grow and thrive and develop, and I got absolute joy out of seeing other people succeed in what they did." – **Antonia**

"I definitely see value in Strengths for students in a huge way. I really feel like that is a special niche that I can speak into, and then feel aligned with on a personal side." – **Anne**

"I want to be able to teach sharing Strengths to the world in a democratic way and a way that feels like it's accessible to everyone." – **Jo**

Finding FISH in a Strengths-Based Practice

Consider your leading strengths themes with the following questions:

* Get stuff done: What do you love being invested in every single day?
* Inspiring others: What legacy would you love to leave that will stand the test of time?
* Connecting to the world around you: In whom would you most like to invest, and why is your service to others so critical to your sense of purpose?
* Thinking: What new knowledge will you create that has the potential to change the world in some small way?
* Create something new: What are you inspired to create, and what is its deeper purpose?

Consider the following questions and how they might help clarify your purpose. **Choose three or four questions** that resonate with you the most to focus on:

* Why is your powerful habit of hard work an essential part of your legacy?
* Why is evidence-based decision making and solving for root cause an essential element of your purpose?
* How will your communication skill help you craft, refine, and articulate a powerful purpose statement?
* Who is your benchmark for building a legacy to be proud of? What can you learn from them?
* What hidden ripples might your sense of purpose reveal in the future?
* How does your sense of justice, equity and fairness inform your purpose?
* How will you build on the historical legacy you have built so far in life for the future?

- Whose lives will you develop over the course of living your purpose?
- Who will you emotionally impact on the journey of creating your legacy?
- How will your integrated purpose shape the future of your life and those you love most?
- Who will you love to include on the journey of fulfilling your legacy?
- How will your archive of resources and information become part of your legacy?
- How will your passion for learning be fulfilled on the journey of building your legacy?
- What problem are you uniquely poised to solve, and how does your practice contribute the best solutions?
- How will your commitment to purpose build the foundation upon which your legacy will be remembered?
- How will your integrated purpose be informed by the energy to meet, engage, and inspire many different people?

The following questions might help lift how you live your purpose every single day. **Choose three or four questions** that resonate most deeply:

- How is 'getting new projects started' critical to the energy of your legacy?
- How does your 'go with the flow' energy allow you to flex your sense of purpose as needed to any situation?
- How does your orchestration of time and resource enable you to fulfil your purpose to a high standard?
- How does your presence and leadership charisma contribute to building your legacy?

Finding FISH in a Strengths-Based Practice

- How will you ensure your purpose is lived carefully and intentionally, with contingencies where necessary?
- How will your love of routine and structure bring you discipline in the way you live your purpose?
- Why does your energy to finish projects give you confidence in your ability to complete your legacy?
- Why will it be essential to create consensus and foster harmony with those who will contribute to your legacy?
- How will you bring variety and creativity to the way you live your purpose fully?
- How will you surround yourself with magically talented people in order to fulfil your legacy?
- How will your thoughtfulness and rich, quality thinking contribute to your sense of purpose?
- Why will your energy for constant and never-ending improvement contribute to your sense of purpose?
- How will your positivity contribute to your resilience when your legacy-building hits a roadblock?
- Who will be in your trusted inner circle as you build your legacy?
- What promises can you make to yourself that will contribute to fulfilling your purpose?
- How will your confidence and certainty help you persevere in building your legacy?
- Why will it be essential to pivot and explore many options in the pursuit of your purpose?

Rather than be the 'right' question for you at this time, the questions above are intended to inspire your thinking and explore different facets of your potential strengths, while ruminating on the topic of integrated purpose. What would be another valuable question you could ask yourself to clarify your integrated purpose, or live your purpose more fully?

Rather than pursuing the 'perfect purpose statement', it is more useful to create a sense of purpose in everything you do, re-writing and re-committing to a purpose statement on a daily, weekly, monthly, yearly, or lifetime basis. Sometimes it is enough for my purpose to be "to walk the dog and clear my head in the fresh air", and "to engage my Connectedness in reflecting on how I fit in the grand scheme of things".

I have written about the evolution of a purpose statement substantially in my first book, *The Joy of Finding FISH*, and my own personal and practice purpose statements have evolved greatly over the last 15 years. These have included:

- To be a great dad, loving husband and extraordinary coach.
- To make dreams come true.

Following the loss of my wife Fiona to cancer in July 2021, a very good friend of mine and fellow Strengths coach (Antonia Milkop) helped me commit to the following purpose:

- To honour Fiona in everything I do.
- To love and support my sons Cameron and Ross unconditionally.
- To live FISH fully and bring FISH to the world.

I am grateful for Antonia's input into my life and practice, and at the time, she did not realise the impact she had with our conversation.

These were the product of necessary segmentation of my purpose during a very difficult time in my life. Very recently, I have invested time and had spontaneous revelations about my integrated purpose. A new integrated purpose statement that I am exploring is:

To experience love in all its forms.

Finding FISH in a Strengths-Based Practice

This is likely to be a topic for a future book, if I have the courage to embrace it.

Purpose is a very personal subject. We are each on our own unique journey. I believe that this is the best time in history to be alive, and it is up to us to make the most of our circumstances. Creating a compelling integrated purpose that plays to your strengths has the potential to bring you a Southern Cross/North Star – that fixed point in the sky to navigate your way through life. If you can express what you want out of this life, and remain focused on bringing that to fruition, you have a very good chance of experiencing fulfilment, inspiration, success, and happiness (FISH) on your own terms.

> *How will an integrated purpose contribute to your experience of FISH?*
>
> *Which of your significant strengths has the most important role to play in creating and living your core purpose?*

CHAPTER 6

Strengths-Based Values

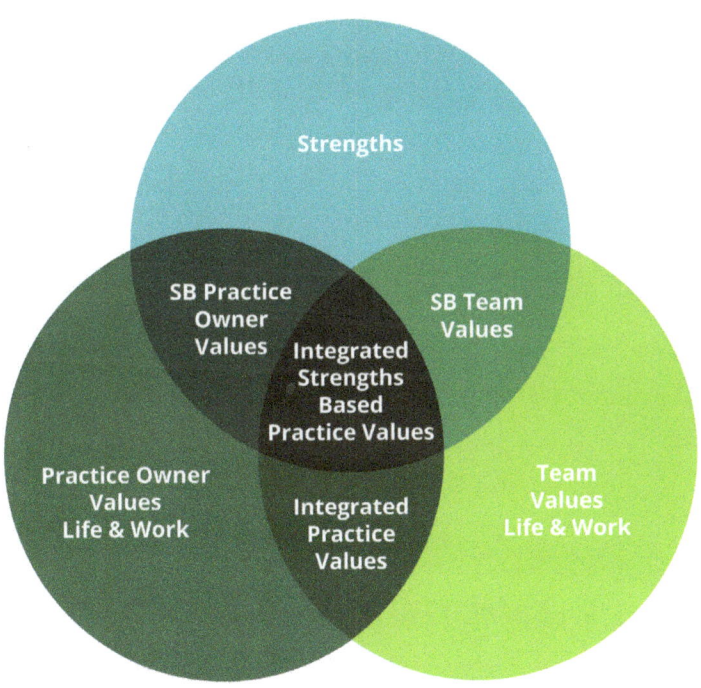

EXPLORING HUMANITY'S CURRENCIES AND VALUES

I'VE BEEN REFLECTING on the differences and similarities between the major currencies of humanity and humanity's shared values. While the latter can almost be infinite, much public writing has defined the four human currencies as time, energy, identity, and money.

It becomes interesting to consider how our behaviours are motivated by currencies and values, and when our actions are in alignment with our words (integrity). Based on the four currencies above, I feel that human behaviour is currently dominated by the pursuit of money in the fastest possible time, and this might be the source of many of the world's challenges right now. Energy and a respect for identity are suffering, with many around the world feeling burnt out and inhibited from expressing the best version of themselves.

Expanding the list of currencies into human values, the following alphabetical list captures some of the dominant hopes and dreams around the world:

Ability	Abundance	Achievement	Attention
Compassion	Connection	Energy	Experiences
Freedom	Fulfilment	Health	Identity
Joy	Knowledge	Love	Money
Success	Time	Wealth	

This is just a small sample of all of the potential values in humanity, which might be defined as 'Everything we individually and collectively love and value in the world'.

Living congruently within a set of core values is potentially a high source of fulfilment, inspiration, success, and happiness (FISH). Think of core values as a set of rules for living life, but you get to set and change the rules whenever you choose! Some people's rules are highly competitive, with themselves if not with other people in their lives, while other individuals may take a more co-operative approach to the rules of the game.

Your core values generally reflect what you care most about in life and work. Values serve you well, until they don't, and often the stress and conflict in a person's life is created by incongruent values. It is also an interesting process to identify how each value is lived on a day-to-day basis, and to understand that this is a very personal and individual choice. One person's definition of balancing family and career is unlikely to be the same for another individual. It is remarkable how many people claim family to be an important core value, and yet choose to spend 60 hours per week running a business or performing in a high-pressure job.

Imagine an individual who sets a high standard for themselves when it comes to health and well-being, but who is also very social and gets a great deal of enjoyment from drinking with friends and family. These two choices may not be in conflict, unless and until the drinking habit becomes an inhibitor to living a life with high health and well-being. Symptoms of a terrible night's sleep, fuzzy thinking the next day, and grumpiness that begins affecting other relationships may all contribute to rethinking the need for alcohol when socialising, or at least taking steps to reduce intake to a moderate level. Just reflecting on whether health and well-being really is more important than socialising is a useful debate to have in order to influence habitual behaviour.

Our values change over a lifetime and can be shaped significantly by the experience of our lives through different moments. For example, during the early phase of a career – prior to starting a family – money, time, and energy might feature highly, while in later years, love, connection, and fulfilment might dominate. Similarly, some of the conflicts between generations can often be explained through the lens of values. Retiring baby-boomers who built careers and lives focused on money, wealth, identity, and ability may not easily understand younger generations who are motivated by fulfilment, experiences, and freedom (I am conscious of making gross generalisations through these observations, and would highlight that baby boomers began their lives with a deep connection to love and freedom during the 1960s).

The people we grow up and surround ourselves with also play a significant role in shaping our values. Parents, siblings, and peers during our younger years may shape our perspectives about success, relationships, and the way we might seek validation from those we love. In particular, parent and grandparent relationships to money, effort, and achievement may influence a young person's choice and commitment to a calling, choice of life partners, and how they measure success through their lifetime.

Friends, peers, and mentors in adult life can also be powerful role models when it comes to living and pursuing our values. At the time of writing this article, I have two inspiring role models influencing the future of my life and my practice. I suspect one leads with money, time, and identity, providing me with a roadmap of how best to expand my personal wealth and find my own formula for self-expression. The other embodies energy, love, and experiences with an amazing level of congruence and consistency with these values. Neither choice of values is right nor wrong, but my awareness of where their major currencies lie helps me make better decisions in my own life and practice.

Reflecting on the most recent years of my life, my own dominant values and currencies are love, fulfilment, and knowledge (though the latter often exchanges with connection when given the opportunity). Family can be a surrogate for love, and I often feel that my relationship with clients and close friends are informed by a very broad definition of family.

My leading value of family has become so much easier to live congruently with since starting my practice in 2017. Prior to that, 22 years of employment in the pharmaceutical and management consulting industries created regular stressful circumstances where I simply could not be in two places at once, and a career responsibility would often overshadow the best interests of my family. Leading a practice and being largely in control of my own commitments has meant being able to prioritise my sons' needs, which have been especially important in light of losing their mother to cancer in 2021.

In running a practice with a small team of support staff including a practice manager and/or executive assistant (usually remotely located), it is important to acknowledge the importance of the practice owner's values as fundamental to how the practice is likely to thrive and grow. In my case, 'Honour the Evolution' and 'Live Life Out Loud' influence both my coaching and mentoring style, and my transparency through social media and newsletters. If my team were uncomfortable with this in any way, we would have a conflict to navigate, given how highly I value these two statements, and how they influence my core behaviour.

The value sets of other members of the practice team are also important in ensuring that the culture of the practice is in alignment with their needs and wishes.

The following interview content reflects the wide variety of ways values play out in a practice context. Some examples relate to choosing core values, while others consider how strengths play a role in living the values on a regular basis.

	Personal Values	Practice Values	Strengths-Based Values
Teri	I think that Self-assurance allows me to talk with people on any level and not feel intimidated by them or uncomfortable about those conversations.	Being Futuristic gets me juiced to do the business development activity. I can see what's going to be on the other side of that activity.	I use my strengths to support my values. One of the questions I ask myself before I go into a client meeting is, "How do I want to show up? How do I want to be generous in this conversation?"
Charlotte	Courage has been a driving force for me personally. Whilst I don't say it's courageous, many people say, "Wow, you moved from the UK to Australia. That's very courageous."	For me the value is relishing every moment, even the moments between clients, when you feel the enormity of what you do for people. If we're going to do something, it needs to be meaningful.	I realised I need to work somewhere with fun, humour, engagement, and obvious linkages with my Positivity, my Woo, my Communication, and the Maximiser.
Murray	My number one Clifton Strengths is Relator. And so if I think about Relator, it's deep, authentic relationships with others, with fewer rather than with lots of people. And so, for me, that Relator helps me to live that honestly.	I see that the values in my practice and the values of who I am as a person are interlinked. If I think about the purpose of my practice, it is about how I can create space for people to grow to be their best selves, and to achieve what they want by being their best selves.	My strengths help me live the values that are important to me; my strengths help me be me. For example, one of my top values is honesty. Honesty is important to me in how I run my business, my practice and my work with my clients and who I am as a person.

Finding FISH in a Strengths-Based Practice

	Personal Values	Practice Values	Strengths-Based Values
Holly	As a person of faith, one of my core values is loving God and loving people. High relationship-building empathy is number one. I care about people; I want to help people.	The courage that goes hand in hand with leading with the truth is where my purpose comes into play. And I do carry that into my business. That's 100% what my business is about, it's about leading with the truth and I use that with my clients all the time.	My Strategic Ideation Maximiser gives me a plan. "How does this sound to you? Would you like to do this?" I am excited for you and want to help you get there. I do it with my kid. I do it with anybody I come in contact with. I can't help but want people to do what makes them happy.
James	My number three value is empathy. That's a big part of sales; understanding what the client is looking for or what interests them.	My personal and business values are trust, authenticity, and integrity. Particularly in an industry that doesn't have a reputation for having those things at the forefront of the industry (art dealership), operating in a trustworthy way is something that I have to do.	In my top 10 strengths, I've got Communication and Individualisation. I have to do these transparently to ensure that there is no betrayal of trust at any point along the way.

IN A LIFE WELL-LIVED

Tash, my practice manager for the last three years, lives on a sailboat in Northland in New Zealand (I live in Wellington). The flexibility of responsibilities coupled with an atmosphere of self-imposed deadlines and 'Work when inspired, the rest of the time, PLAY' means that we are both productive, but neither is overly dependent on the other for inputs or outputs. Similarly, following an 'Every day is a seven-day weekend' philosophy creates maximum use of the week and we are both used to exchanging 'work' communication at odd times of the day or week.

Tash's reflections on our shared practice values are an example of how values play out in the way we live day to day:

"Firstly, 'Do what I love and love what I do' is a motto that speaks to my heart. It's all about finding that sweet spot where our passions and strengths intersect. I wholeheartedly believe that when we're doing work we love, it's not just a job anymore; it becomes a source of joy and fulfilment. And it's a philosophy that speaks to what you do, and I wholeheartedly align with it!

Living our 'why' and helping others find theirs is also something I hold dear. Discovering purpose (something that I am still journeying forth with) is so important. It's amazing to be a small part of the story with you helping others discover their true purpose and values.

'Every week is a seven-day weekend.' Oh, how I resonate with that sentiment! Work-life balance is a priority for me, and I firmly believe that life should be filled with enjoyment, relaxation, and adventure outside of work. Embracing the idea that our time off is just as valuable as my time on the clock allows us to recharge and bring our best selves to our work.

'Work when inspired; the rest of the time, play!' What a wonderful approach! I completely agree that our creativity and productivity soar when we're in the flow.

Lastly, transparency, confidentiality, and fairness are values I deeply appreciate (this is probably the top on my list in terms of transparency). I deeply feel injustice (hence my work in a non-profit space!) and believe that honouring equality and transparency is something I try and take with me daily.

I'm excited about the journey ahead and the opportunity to make dreams come true, live life out loud, and embrace both personal and professional growth.

Thank you for being you and fostering a culture that embraces these values.

Warm regards,

Tash"

It is interesting to reflect on the added impact of taking a Strengths-Based approach to establishing and living values every day. Based on the five categories of Strengths previously discussed, here are a few Strengths-Based values questions to consider:

- CREATE something new – how might your values reflect the need to produce something creatively (through art, dance, music, writing, wealth, business/practice legacy, etc.)?
- INSPIRE yourself or others – how might your service to or influence of others be reflected in one or more of your values?
- CONNECT to the world – who are the most important people in your life and how are they represented within your value set?
- THINKING style – how is knowledge or wisdom represented in your values?
- GET STUFF DONE – in what ways are productivity and achievement reflected in your values?

Strengths-Based questions to help build your core values. If a question doesn't resonate, skip over it, as it probably refers to a non-strength of yours:

- Which of your strengths are fundamental to or fundamentally linked to your core values in life or work?
- What do you care most about in life and at work?
- How are your core values reflected in the core principles of how you choose to live your life?
- How will your focus on achievement be reflected in one or more of your values?
- How will your starter energy and momentum be acknowledged in your values?
- How will your list of core values reflect your ability to 'go with the flow' in most situations?
- How will your analytical abilities be reflected in one or more of your core values?
- How is your natural presence and leadership reflected in one or more of your core values?
- How might the spiritual and/or practical side of Connectedness inform your choice of core values?
- How is your sense of justice, equity, and fairness fundamental to your choice of core values?
- In what way does your personal history inform your current core values?
- How might caution and risk awareness be reflected in your core values?
- How will your energy to develop yourself and others be reflected in your core values?
- In what way will caring/feeling for others be reflected in your core values?

Finding FISH in a Strengths-Based Practice

- How might your energy for completing be reflected in your choice of core values?
- Why is building consensus with those around you important in your choice of core values?
- How might your ability to generate a huge variety of ideas contribute to your variety of core values?
- How might your appreciation for the diverse talent of those around you be reflected in your core values?
- How might information/knowledge gathering, archiving, and sharing be a fundamental element of one or more of your values?
- How will your journey of passionate learning be reflected in your core values?
- In what way will your energy for constant and never-ending improvement be reflected in your core values?
- How do your core values reflect your intention and talent for solving problems consistently?
- How will your energy to inspire and positively influence the people around you be reflected in your core values?

Strengths-Based Values questions that help you live your values every day. If a question doesn't resonate, skip over it, as it probably refers to a non-strength of yours:

- How will you make it easy to live by your core values on a day-to-day basis?
- How might your orchestration skills help you balance all of your core values while navigating life?
- How can you use your communication skills to ensure everyone around you is clear about the values you live by?
- Which of your role models share your core values?
- How will the rhythm of your life be reflected in your core values?

- How might you ensure that your core values will stand the test of time?
- In what way might your values reflect your positive inclusive energy?
- How might you prioritise reflection time as part of your core values?
- How will your sense of optimism and positivity influence the expression of all of your core values?
- With whom from your inner circle will you share your core values?
- How will you ensure that your core values represent a supportive and helpful promise to yourself in the way you live your life?
- Where might your confidence be reflected in your core values?
- How will your core values give you energy and boundaries in the fulfilment of your legacy?
- How might you articulate your core values in a way that maximises the options available to you in any situation?

Like purpose, core values are very personal. There is no right or wrong answer, only a sense that a value 'feels right' for you and, more importantly, serves you well in living a life well-lived.

This chapter was intended to emphasise the value and variety of strategies for creating a value set. It was written to encourage you to become more intentional about how you create and live your values on a daily basis. Values are often our 'rulebook for life'. They reflect how we react to and navigate situations over time to identify our preferences and where our character meets the chaos of the world around us. The breakdown of a relationship, or dissatisfaction with a workplace situation can almost always be explained by an incongruence of values.

As you reflect on your own currencies and values, how might you answer the following questions?

Finding FISH in a Strengths-Based Practice

Based on your behaviours (not what you wish to be true), which currencies are most important to you?

What do you love and care about most in your life? How do your actions reflect this?

How might clarity of Strengths-Based values lift your experience of fulfilment, inspiration, success, and happiness (FISH)?

Which of your core strengths are fundamental to living your values consistently?

CHAPTER 7

Strengths-Based Relationships

*"The quality of your life is
the quality of your relationships."*

Tony Robbins

FULFILMENT, INSPIRATION…

Christopher			Tash
Always looking to improve the practice, my performance, and the lives/ businesses/ practices of clients.	**Maximiser** ←	**Achiever** →	Not shy about, and enjoys working hard; nothing seems too much of an effort.
Not afraid to take on a new challenge where learning is required.	**Learner** ←	**Ideation** →	Lots of ideas on how to develop and improve the practice; really great at coming up with multiple approaches to solve the same problem.
Sees the big picture and values the 'ripple effect' of client impact.	**Connectedness** ←	**Strategic** →	Great at contingency planning and finding lots of different ways forward.
Collects, organises, archives, and retrieves useful information in the service of others.	**Input** ←	**Input** →	Wealth of technology-based resources, project planning platforms, and identifying just the right option to solve a problem.
Sees interaction with people as a source of energy and momentum; comfortable public speaking/ presenting.	**Woo** ←	**Arranger** →	Coupled with Achiever, orchestrates multiple projects seamlessly and thrives when many plates are spinning.

Finding FISH in a Strengths-Based Practice

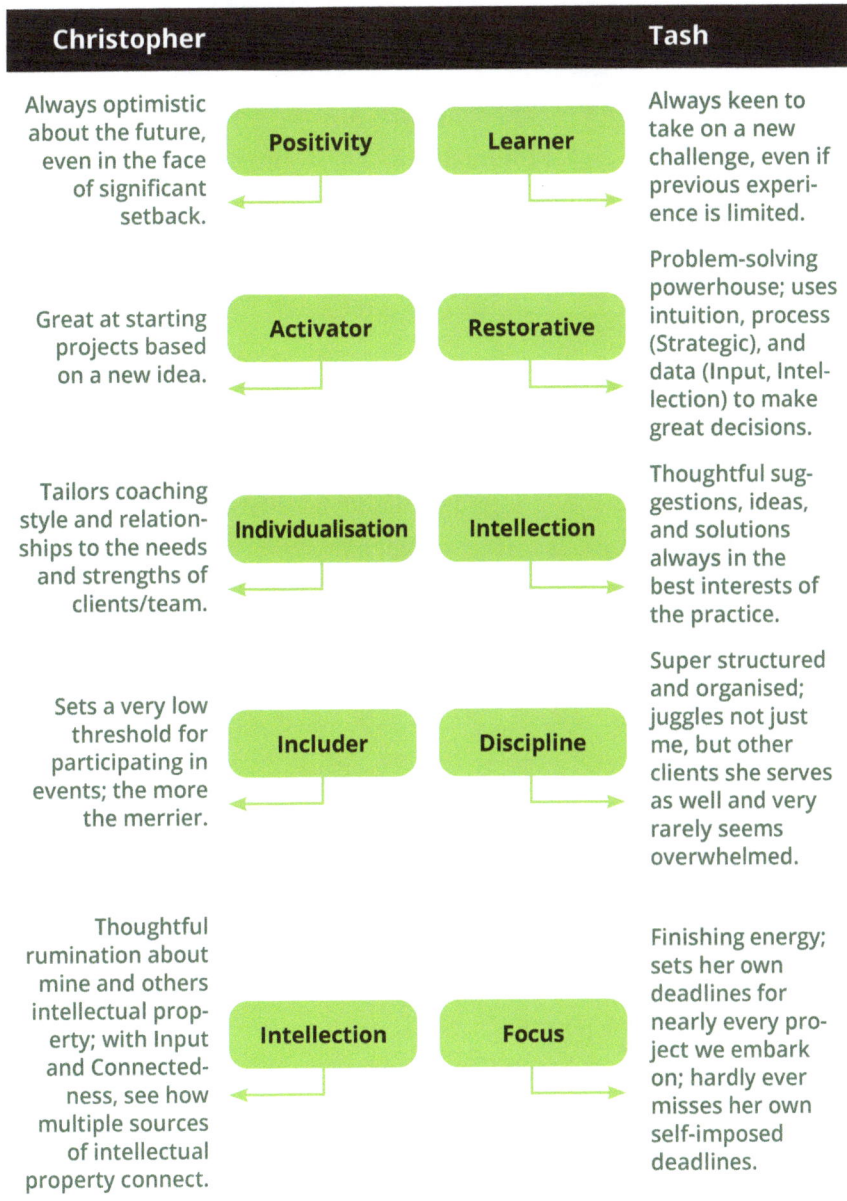

IN A LIFE WELL-LIVED

Complementary partnerships are at the very heart of a Strengths-Based philosophy. Great teamwork comes from a beautiful alignment of what each person loves most and does best with shared and individual responsibilities. In turn, that creates a much greater outcome than any one individual can achieve. In the absence of a Strengths-Based approach, relationships can often be strained or break down entirely due to a lack of appreciation for the differences between two people. The most powerful partnerships occur when two people with exceptionally different talents work together beautifully to achieve something exponentially greater than either could do on their own.

I am blessed to have found an amazing practice manager, Tash Nihill, who is extraordinary at nearly everything I am bad at. Our relationship works so well in part because my complementary talents are not in domains where Tash would necessarily thrive. Our partnership is built on trust and respect, for our differences as much as for our similarities, and we share a sense of purpose and values that make it easy to show up at work every day.

The table and insights on the preceding pages outline some of the ways we leverage our strengths within our practice partnership, effectively building a strong wall or foundation. Definitions are our own, rather than Gallup's official definitions.

One of the most powerful complementary partnerships among all of the practice owners I interviewed was the team at Hatch Talent: Julie Brophy and Michelle Burman. During the interview, their partnership was awesome to witness. They were consciously competent about their Strengths relationship, and seamlessly answered the interview questions. Each person contributed a rich opinion about their partnership, and they often finished each other's sentences throughout the interview. It left me feeling that there was something very special and almost magical about their friendship and business relationship.

Finding FISH in a Strengths-Based Practice

Here is a sample of content from their interview:

Julie: What we've been doing for the last five years has very much been responding to the needs that our clients have at the moment. I would love us to move into a more proactive space.

> **Michelle:** *I want to create ripples in the world through the work I do with coaching and training.*

The value that has been our foundation for Hatch has always been our relationship and its well-being. When we think about how our strengths have influenced that, Michelle and I have key relationship-building themes. My key relationship theme is Connectedness. That sense of trust, having each other's backs, and being connected. Michelle, for you, what do you think about?

> *So there are a few values I think of; they definitely include the value of my relationship with Julie. When we started this business we agreed, no matter what happens, we must not put our friendship at risk. We were determined to be best friends who can create something significant together, but never to the detriment of our friendship. I would summarise all of that in the word 'love'.*

That is our primary value. It is the love and respect that we have for each other. Michelle and I have different strengths. For example, Michelle is positive. I'm an achiever, and I don't need fun, or I don't realise I need fun until I've been without it for so long. I can grind, grind, finish the week, grind, grind, grind. And Michelle has this beautiful ability to bring fun and light-heartedness to things. That was something I didn't even know I needed.

> *And it's Julie's focus that enables us to go after things; she truly embodies being an achiever, she has this wonderful drive and energy and stamina. Our strengths nicely complement each other.*

We will always share our successes with one another, but also our challenges as well. It's not a structure we have set in stone, it's just that when we have a heart-warming conversation or facilitate something that I know landed well, straightaway I share that with Michelle, and she with me.

> *We both are always learning, that is always rich for us. We're also recovering perfectionists, we're working together to embrace a growth mindset.*

I think one of the things we didn't even realise when we started the business is that we're complementary in that Michelle loves facilitation, but for me that's second to coaching. This has been very helpful. Michelle is also a quicker thinker, and I'm more likely to go abstract.

> *I think fast but I don't think as deep as Julie, so I might be fast but the beauty comes when we marry it together. We'll be talking about something and the next morning she'll be able to deepen the thoughts and ideas we had, I'm very thankful for that.*

Finding FISH in a Strengths-Based Practice

The power of Julie and Michelle's relationship perhaps lies in the seamless way their talents hand over to each other or combine to create amazing outcomes in their lives as well as in their practice. While the relationship was founded in natural connection, they have also invested in each other over time to make their partnership even stronger. Often, a new working relationship starts out strong, but then we fail to nurture it to the potential it deserves. The more intentional this kind of Strengths-Based partnership, the stronger the relationship can become.

Here's a look at Julie and Michelle's complementary strengths, and how they build their wall together.

FULFILMENT, INSPIRATION...

Julie	Michelle
Julie brings endless energy to her life – she is a role model for me. I love the fact that she helps us turn ideas into actions that can be completed – enabling us to achieve our goals.	**Achiever** ↔ **Positivity** Michelle almost always believes that something will work – whether in our business or personal lives.
Julie's incredible open-mindedness and curiosity continually lead her to discover ideas and approaches that positively impact our clients and our own business.	**Learner** ↔ **Woo** Michelle loves meeting new people, meaning facilitation and coaching are a joy.
In tandem with her Learner, Julie's Thirst for Knowledge provides fantastic ingredients for her Intellection to ponder. The combination of these three thinking themes provides us with a massive competitive advantage.	**Input** ↔ **Input** As we both have this strength, we share a love of books, articles, podcasts, etc. and there's no-one better to have a robust conversation about a range of psychology and wellbeing approaches. It's probably the strength that initially consolidated our friendship beyond the usual professional boundaries.

80 SUCCESS AND HAPPINESS...

Finding FISH in a Strengths-Based Practice

Julie			Michelle
I am in awe of Julie's ability to connect ideas together and come up with new and creative ways to get things done. She also uses her Connectedness to build relationships in all areas of her life.	**Connectedness** ←	→ **Communication**	Michelle has such ease when it comes to putting complex thoughts into words – it's something I try to emulate but it doesn't come as naturally. She always has little stories to share that are both fun and funny.
I constantly rely on the depth of Julie's thinking – we may discuss a concept and her beautiful Intellection will deepen and broaden our thinking. This improves our offerings to our clients.	**Intellection** ←	→ **Restorative**	This strength helps us to pick up little things that might not be working as well in our material – perhaps we could adjust the sequence of the supporting materials. Michelle's Restorative would never allow the work we produce to become stale.
Julie is our role model for actually following through on what we commit to! Her ability to create goals, prioritise, and then persevere is exemplary. It's a life saver given I have no Focus!	**Focus** ←	→ **Individualisation**	Michelle's fascination with psychology has led to her completing her Bachelor of Science in Psych and now MScience in Organisational Psychology which, of course, adds a great amount of depth to our offering.

FULFILMENT, INSPIRATION...

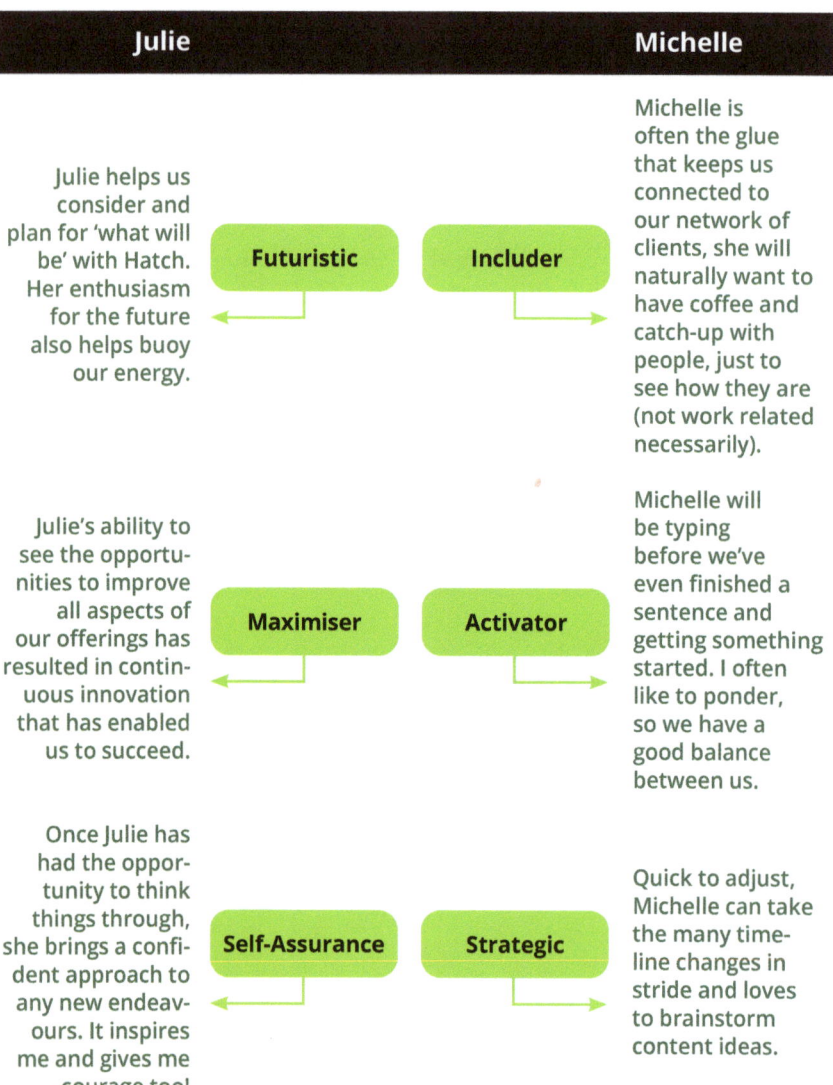

Finding FISH in a Strengths-Based Practice

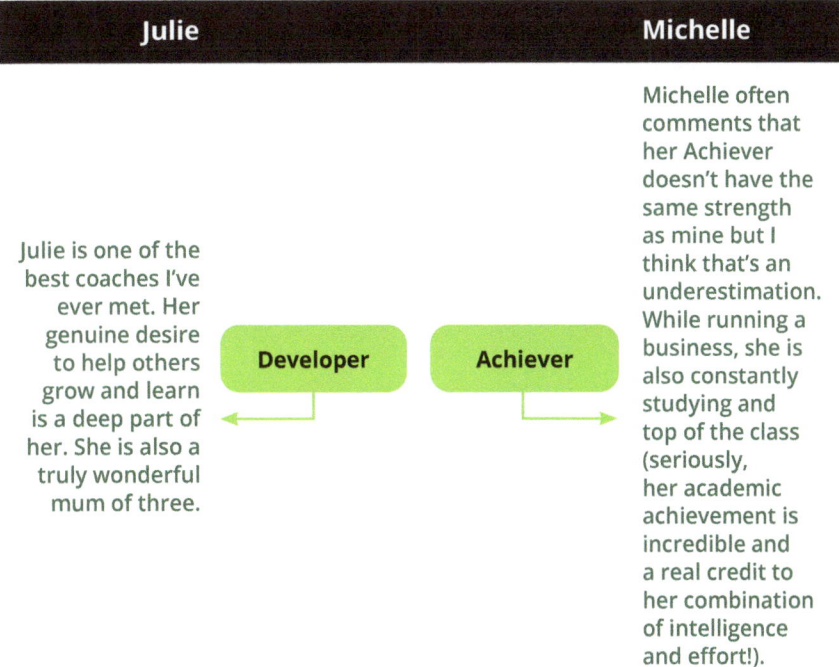

Julie	Michelle
Julie is one of the best coaches I've ever met. Her genuine desire to help others grow and learn is a deep part of her. She is also a truly wonderful mum of three.	Michelle often comments that her Achiever doesn't have the same strength as mine but I think that's an underestimation. While running a business, she is also constantly studying and top of the class (seriously, her academic achievement is incredible and a real credit to her combination of intelligence and effort!).

Here are some Strengths-Based partnership questions to consider:

- Who are the most important people in your life and at work?
- Do you have a good feel for their strengths and how these complement your own?
- When do your strengths combinations leverage off each other?
- When do they come into conflict?
- What strength would you love to discover in someone new that you definitely don't have in your dominant themes?

How will taking a conscious approach to Strengths-Based partnerships help lift your experience of fulfilment, inspiration, success, and happiness (FISH)?

Which of your many strengths do you use most to forge strong relationships?

CHAPTER 8

Strengths-Based Leadership

*"Leadership is not about being in charge.
It is about taking care of those in your charge."*

Simon Sinek

This chapter is significantly inspired by *Strengths-Based Leadership* by Tom Rath (Gallup), which is one of my favourite books created within the Strengths movement. Its genius is the positioning of Strengths/talents in the **context** of leadership, and the insights it provides in leadership styles, the needs of followers, and the relationship between great leadership and the well-being and thriving of followers.

LEADERSHIP STYLES

Extrapolating from the five categories of strengths from the "Introduction to Strengths" chapter, the following might be a useful description for some of the dominant styles of leadership:

- GET STUFF DONE – **Lead by example**
    - Do what you say you're going to do; keep promises; deliver productive contribution alongside followers.
    - How does your reputation for high delivery and getting things done earn the respect of followers?

- INSPIRE yourself or others – **Lead from the stage**
    - Great storytelling; charisma and persuasion; deliver hope (especially if backed up by substance).
    - How is your magical storytelling compelling and persuasive?

- CONNECT to the world – **Lead from the heart**
    - Understand your audience; walk in another person's shoes; shared emotion.

- How does your deep understanding of your followers contribute to your style of leadership?

* THINK – **Thought leadership**
  - Robust thinking/planning; intelligent and strategic; unique ideas that inspire.
  - What would you like to be known for?

* CREATE something new – **Lead through creation**
  - Tangible services or products that meet new needs; new systems and processes that bring stability and efficiency.
  - What can you create that would bring maximum benefit to your followers?

Understanding the categories above speaks to the relevance of authenticity. You can imagine a leader who pretends to be something they are not because they think that is what's expected. If my natural talent is in the domain of thought leadership and leading from the heart, why would I present to a large audience my compelling story, when I would have a much greater impact hosting focus groups and creating the intimacy of rich personal conversations about a topic I am passionate about or an expert in? Similarly, if I am comfortable leading through creation and leading by example, my approach with followers could be co-creation workshops with specific, tangible outcomes in mind. If I fall into the trap of pretending to be something I'm not, my followers will see right through me and become disenchanted rather quickly.

In the context of leading a Strengths-Based Practice, there are at least two constituent follower groups to consider – the internal team and clients. The internal team (practice manager, executive assistant, relevant outsource partners) will benefit from understanding the leadership preferences of the practice owner. This may assist with determining practice strategy, client impact, and modes of delivery, which will be described in the next chapter. For example, a practice strategy leveraging the practice owner's strength in leading from the stage may unlock lots of potential with a speaking strategy, either to create leads for other delivery modes, or create substantial income from the power of inspiring speaking.

In contrast, a practice owner who is exceptional in thought leadership or leading through creation may get on a roll with authoring (books, white papers, social media) or creating rich content for training programmes. It is important to note that most people have two or more leadership styles that they can access with a high level of impact, so it would be very rare to limit your tactical choices to just one leadership style.

When a practice owner leads from the heart (connection), they will likely build a very loyal, trust-based following, with both their internal team and with external clients. This can often weather difficult storms when relationships are challenged or frayed. Similarly, if the practice owner leads through inspiration, they may be in a position to motivate an internal team to achieve extraordinary things based on their talent, AND inspire clients to change their life or their business for the better.

FOUR NEEDS OF FOLLOWERS

One of the most powerful pieces of leadership research that I have ever seen reported is Gallup's study, *The Four Needs of Followers*. In the simplest terms, Gallup went out to thousands of followers around the world and asked them what they needed from their leaders. They compiled all the answers, themed and coded thousands of transcripts, and were able to summarise the results into four clear themes:

- Hope
- Trust
- Stability
- Compassion

Finding FISH in a Strengths-Based Practice

I genuinely believe these four words have the potential to change the world – especially the world of work – significantly. Based on your own experience, for every negative leadership role model you can think of, I am betting that one or more of these four needs was absent from the relationship of that leader with their followers. On the other hand, exceptional leadership can be characterised by a leader's ability to fulfil all of these needs, often at different times in their tenure as leader. The most public recent example of a leader living these four needs wholeheartedly is Jacinda Ardern, Prime Minister of New Zealand. Regardless of political persuasion, most people had a high level of respect for the job she did over her six-year tenure as leader of the country. Some of the examples of supporting followers in their needs included:

- Hope – an enormous level of personal public communication through the Covid-19 crisis, with clarity about future contingencies.
- Trust – transparency often even when the future was uncertain.
- Stability – core ministers remained relatively stable over the six-year tenure, creating predictability within government decision making.
- Compassion – a very personal and emotional response to the massacre in Christchurch, which led to substantial legislative action to restrict guns in New Zealand.

Often when leadership goes wrong, the paradigm for success is defined very differently. The currency for success might be financial, power, or status. These are not necessarily the motivation of the leader, but rather the leader's perception of what followers want out of work or life. Loved leaders (think Gandhi, Diana, Mandela, etc.) all choose currencies that are more connected to the human condition (peace, compassion, freedom) rather than external sources of hierarchy.

In leading a Strengths-Based Practice, how might these four needs provide relevance and context in your leadership of your team and clients? Which need are you fulfilling on any given day, or with any given intervention?

Before you move on, reflect on the following:

- Which of the Four Needs of Followers are you most in need of right now?
- Which of the Four Needs of Followers do you suspect is a leadership strength of yours?

Based on your answers, consider the following Four Needs of Followers Matrix, circle where your greatest need of followers lies, and where you feel is your greatest leadership ability – at the intersection of these circles should be language that resonates with you, and how you might want to focus your energy:

	Follower's Need for Hope	Follower's Need for Trust	Follower's Need for Stability	Follower's Need for Compassion
Leader's Ability to Inspire Hope	Shared Vision	Trust in a Better Future	Hope for a More Stable Future	Inspire a Kinder Future
Leader's Ability to Inspire Trust	Trust in a Brighter Future	Reciprocal Integrity	Trust in a More Stable Future	Trust & Commitment to Kindness
Leader's Ability to Inspire Stability	Predictable Plan for a Brighter Future	Trust Consistency	Solid Foundations & Shared Certainty	Systems & Structures to Live & Work Compassionately
Leader's Ability to Inspire Compassion	Deep Caring for a Brighter Future	Care and Commitment to do What We Say We Will Do	Care for the Well-Being of Followers Through Solid Foundations	Deep Caring for People First

It might be valuable to repeat this exercise with your practice team and/or with a few highly trusted clients.

This model can be taken a step further. One of my favourite business development books, particularly in the context of large corporates, is *Good to Great* by Jim Collins. The power behind this book is the extraordinary level of research that went into its development. Jim and his team reviewed exceptional businesses in a variety of industries, and then compared each high performer with the rest of the players in their specific industry in order to identify what characteristics separated the good from the great. The timing of the research several decades ago means that while some of the individual case studies may now be out of date, the conclusions that the author and research team arrived at remain relevant today and I believe offer insight to a Strengths-Based Practice, especially as it evolves and matures.

Four of the leadership principles identified to have differentiated the great from the good included:

- Vision – compelling and inspiring vision of the future, usually in the form of a Big Hairy Audacious Goal (BHAG) – measurable and time-bound.
- Brand – who we are as a company; what we stand for; what energy we embody.
- Values – set of rules or principles to live by every day; how we treat each other and our customers.
- Purpose – clear reason to exist; a big 'Why' that could still be true hundreds of years into the future.

Visually, this leadership model can be summarised as:

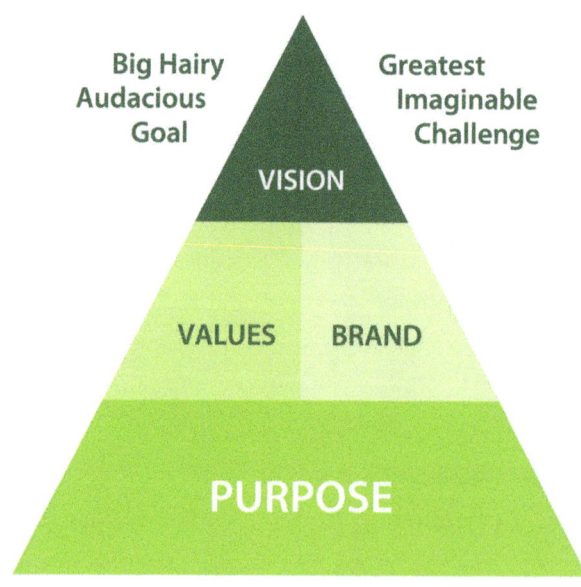

Finding FISH in a Strengths-Based Practice

Based on this model, which element of the pyramid are you likely to be most proficient at leading?

* Vision
* Brand
* Values
* Purpose

What is the greatest need of your followers at the moment (either your practice team, or your most important clients right now)?

* Hope
* Trust
* Stability
* Compassion

Based on your answers, use the following Leadership Matrix to determine the language and energy that your leadership style might benefit most from right now.

	Hope	Trust	Stability	Compassion
Purpose	North Star	Shared Why	Bedrock	Serve Others
Values	Future Standards	Integrity	Authenticity	Care for Others
Vision	Future Legacy	Shared Dreams	Build a Plan	Shared Journey/ Experiences
Brand	Growth	Reputation	Dependability	Stewardship

The Four Needs of Followers Matrix and the Leadership Matrix above are intended to provide new and intentional language to use when communicating with followers. It may be helpful to consider your top two leadership styles and the top two needs of followers to build more variety into your communications.

It is worth reflecting on the potential for a leadership strength to expand and ignite positioning, and contribute to what you become known for. Continuing to invest in self-awareness, and working on improving an already exceptional skill or attribute may be the key to unlocking unlimited potential.

> *Which leadership strengths (Vision/Brand/Values/Purpose/Hope/Trust/Stability/Compassion) have the highest potential to contribute to your experience of fulfilment, inspiration, success, and happiness (FISH)?*
>
> *How will you find a way to fulfil your own needs of followers?*
>
> *What brings you Hope, Trust, Stability, and Compassion in life and running your practice?*

CHAPTER 9

Strengths-Based Thought Leadership

"I am so clever that sometimes I don't understand a single word of what I am saying."

Oscar Wilde

FULFILMENT, INSPIRATION...

While I am an avid reader, I recognise that it is rare to come across a book that changes the trajectory of your life. Three books that fall into this category for me are:

- *The Seven Habits of Highly Effective People* by Stephen Covey, which helped me create positive intention around living a life well-lived.
- *Coaching for Performance* by Sir John Whitmore, which inspired me to leave a 12-year career in pharmaceutical and biotech marketing to pursue a career as a personal and business development coach.
- *The Thought Leaders Practice* by Matt Church, Peter Cook, and Scott Stein made me expand my awareness about becoming a thought leader (beyond being a coach) and running a practice (rather than a business).

This chapter is based on the third book in this list, and I hope to expand the body of knowledge created by the Thought Leaders community by applying a Strengths lens to some of the principles and frameworks that are the foundations of running a thought leaders practice.

Core to building a thought leaders practice is the creation of clusters, or the integration of message, market, and method in order to launch an offer into your chosen marketplace. Chapter Two of *The Thought Leaders Practice* goes into detail around the creation of clusters. It outlines the value of understanding perspective, problems, and preferences that are aligned with a chosen message for a given market and delivered through a specific mode.

What becomes interesting to consider is the impact of Strengths on the choice and execution of message, market, and method. For additional context, method refers to modes of delivery and includes facilitation,

Finding FISH in a Strengths-Based Practice

coaching, training, mentoring, speaking, and authoring, all of which will be explored in more detail in the 'Strengths-Based Delivery' chapter later in this book.

The following table offers a perspective about how each of the five categories of Strengths might be leveraged in the implementation of message, market, and method.

	Message	Market	Method
GET STUFF DONE!	Productivity IS the point!	Markets who admire and value your effort.	Complex programmes delivered seamlessly and made to look easy.
INSPIRE yourself or others	Build reputation on your ability to inspire!	Wowing an audience every time because of your power to persuade.	One to many delivery likely to be more powerful than one on one.
CONNECT to the world around you	How might trust become a fundamental character of your connections?	Who trusts you the most and values your wisdom?	One on one may offer deeper trust than one to many.
THINK	Rigorous and elegant thinking.	Find markets that value the quality of your thinking.	Rich and diverse thinking through multiple modes.
CREATE something new	Build something new and of value, even if simple and incremental.	Create to dazzle your chosen market(s).	Unique delivery as much as unique content.

Similar to the cluster strategy described above, the Thought Leaders community are also obsessed (in a good way!) with the energy to think, sell, and deliver. The table below highlights a Strengths perspective in executing each of these core activities and are expanded upon in later chapters.

FULFILMENT, INSPIRATION...

	Think	Sell	Deliver
GET STUFF DONE!	How can you leverage your work ethic and organisational skills in the creation, storage, and retrieval of your intellectual property (pink and green sheets)?	How will your work ethic and efficiency contribute to the way you hunt for and schedule selling opportunities?	Why will your delivery experiences be as well known for their flow/structure as for their content?
INSPIRE yourself or others	Which of your IP topics are you most passionate about and how do you convey that passion?	Why are you so effective in communicating the change you can create for a prospect?	Which of the six modes of delivery are you most inspired by?
CONNECT to the world around you	Which of your IP will create the most new connections in your chosen market(s)?	How will you leverage your power to connect during sales conversations?	How will you leverage your ability to connect and your ability to create connections for others through your choice of mode(s)?
THINK	What can you do to take your thinking to another level?	In what way will your sales conversations have intellectual rigour?	Which mode of delivery has the potential to showcase your IP in the most impactful way?
CREATE something new	What service/product offering can you create from your best IP?	What could you create that might make the sales process easier or more impactful?	What experience could you create that combines one or more of the delivery modes?

Finding FISH in a Strengths-Based Practice

The intent here is to build a high level of awareness about your preferences and where you might generate the greatest impact through your natural talents. Rather than aiming to be well-rounded, aim to be good enough in most categories and really exceptional (world-class) at a few.

In my own case, I tend to do my best thinking and selling during delivery, and my delivery modes of choice are coaching and authoring. As a result, I have built systems such as recording all of my virtual coaching sessions, and always having a new invitation to work together at the end of a workshop. I am also not afraid to experiment, especially with my most loyal clients. I have developed a 'Let's Talk Love' Card Deck (authoring) which I am testing with my most trusted friends, family, and clients.

> *Which of the following has the potential to contribute most to your experience of fulfilment, inspiration, success, and happiness (FISH)?*
>
> - *Applying your strengths to the cluster strategy – message/market/mode*
> - *Playing to your strengths within think/sell/deliver*
>
> *What are you inspired to DO in your practice as a result of this chapter?*

PART III

Finding Rhythm

*"Rhythm is everything in boxing.
Every move you make starts with your heart,
and that's in rhythm or you're in trouble."*

Sugar Ray Robinson

Living a life well-lived can feel stressful and a bit frenetic perhaps until we find a smooth rhythm to our lives. Identifying the most important experiences we want to have, and then prioritising the fulfilment of these experiences is at the heart of leading a life by design (inspired by *Thought Leaders*). It's interesting to clarify which experiences are repeated for pleasure in a rhythm of days, weeks, months, or years, and which experiences we allow to be spontaneous moments of rapture, to be remembered over a lifetime.

Stephen Covey (*Seven Habits of Highly Effective People; First Things First*) has written extensively about personal effectiveness and prioritisation. One of the most memorable stories he told was about a professor at the front of a class.

The professor holds up a jar full of large rocks and asks the class, "Is the jar full?" receiving a mostly 'yes' response. From under the desk, the professor pulls out a jar of pebbles and slowly pours the pebbles into the jar with the rocks, filling all the gaps between the rocks. They ask again, "Is the jar full?" Less certain now, the class answers with a mixed response.

The professor pulls a jar of sand from under the desk and slowly pours the sand into the jar with the big rocks and the pebbles until no more can fit. The professor asks again, "Is the jar full?" Most of the class respond with a resounding 'yes'. The professor pulls one last jar from under their desk and proceeds to pour water from it, which takes up the space between the sand, the pebbles, and the big rocks, until the jar is well-and-truly full.

The professor then asks, "What if I had started with the water?"

PLANNING OVER TIME – YOUR BIG ROCKS

Unless you begin with the big rocks first, you will never fit everything in. The same applies to life: plan and schedule the big rocks of your life first; the sand and water will always find a way to fit around the big rocks!

Human beings are notoriously bad at committing to and scheduling the 'big rocks' in their life. As a result, the tide of daily activities pushes them from week to week and month to month until they feel exhausted or burnt out.

The joy of running a Strengths-Based Practice is having the luxury of being in complete control of your calendar and the priorities you schedule throughout your year, month, week, or day. The most successful practice owners I've had the pleasure of getting to know are extremely intentional with their time, and start their year by blocking the most important events that will take place, especially involving the most important people in their lives. This might include family holidays, school holidays, professional development investment, and time for self-care.

The rhythm of the practice is also up to the practice owner and might include specific months (work 10 months of the year), specific weeks (week one for selling, weeks two and three for delivery, week four for practice development), or even specific days (Monday practice development, Tuesday to Thursday delivery, Friday selling). The point here is not to advocate a specific rhythm, but to highlight that the practice owner and their team are in complete control of the schedule and can invest in activity when their energies are highest.

Lisa O'Neill, the former amazing CEO of Thought Leaders Business School, has mastered the process of planning and prioritisation to the point that she now publishes her own diary called the *Purpose Planner*. To use Lisa's turn of phrase, her Purpose Planner is "f#$king awesome", starting with its size – hard-bound A4 and seriously thick as each double page spread features half a week. The genius of her planner is that it invites you to set your purpose for the year, for each month, for the week, and even daily. The whole calendar is structured to get you to think about your big rocks on the horizon, whatever your timeline.

ENERGY MANAGEMENT

Along with scheduling and prioritisation, energy management becomes an essential ingredient for running a successful Strengths-Based Practice. Different elements of running the practice will take different levels of energy, and all of this may be influenced by the overall health and wellbeing of the practice owner and their team. Getting sick or run down due to the volume of work is not in the best interests of the practice, nor the reputation of the practice owner.

One aspect of my life that complicates my own Strengths-Based Practice is the fact that I was diagnosed as bipolar in 2009. Thankfully, I acclimatised to two very effective medications soon after my diagnosis and have remained largely stable and symptom-free over more than a decade. My condition is characterised by mood and energy swings from depression (occasionally significant) to elevated thinking and mania (rarer). Sometimes a shift in mood/energy occurs like seasons in the year, or can happen as quickly as within a day. This requires a lot of self-awareness and self-management to function smoothly both professionally and in general life.

The last three years have also been traumatic as my wife was diagnosed with a brain tumour in June 2020 and passed away in July 2021. My experience of grief was profound, and it felt not dissimilar to some periods of depression I had experienced earlier in life. My mood and energy while grieving had a significant effect on what I had capacity for, and what activities could be performed to a reasonable standard.

The chart on the next page outlines my ability to function to a high standard, even when not feeling 100 percent. Regardless of whether you

Finding FISH in a Strengths-Based Practice

have a health condition or other commitments that result in below-normal performance, you may have natural shifts in energy that require you to filter your activities based on those you feel most capable of completing to an acceptable standard.

The point with this table is not to reserve certain activities for when I am at or below a certain energy threshold. And it's certainly not to say I only give a certain percentage of energy to some activities! Rather, it's to know that at any given energy level, there are productive activities I can invest in and keep making progress in my life and practice. The thresholds for various activities are largely determined by my experience and effective systems I have put in place to maintain a certain standard associated with each activity.

For example, my coaching capability and impact is sustained at a pretty high standard, even when my energy is down at 50 percent. This is largely due to the number of years I've been doing it and the specific structure I bring to my coaching sessions. This acts like a safety net when I may not be feeling 100 percent.

What is also true of the table above is that when I am performing at 100 percent or 110 percent, the activities that benefit the most from my good health and strong capacity are the activities that feature lower down the list. So, when I am 110 percent, my ability to tweak and improve existing intellectual property (which I can do well down at 40 percent) is firing on a level that brings deep creativity and potential client impact.

I have found that even when I am really low (20 percent), my ability to parent effectively remains very high, driven by my sense of purpose and the significance I place on being a great dad. My energy for self-preservation, and my commitment to my sons means that I will invest every piece of remaining energy into ensuring their lives are as stable and normal as possible. When I have more energy, the creativity and emotional engagement with my family is higher, and I can stretch my activities. For example, my son Ross is a competitive diver. When I am in a low state, I do everything I can to help him feel confident and ready

FULFILMENT, INSPIRATION...

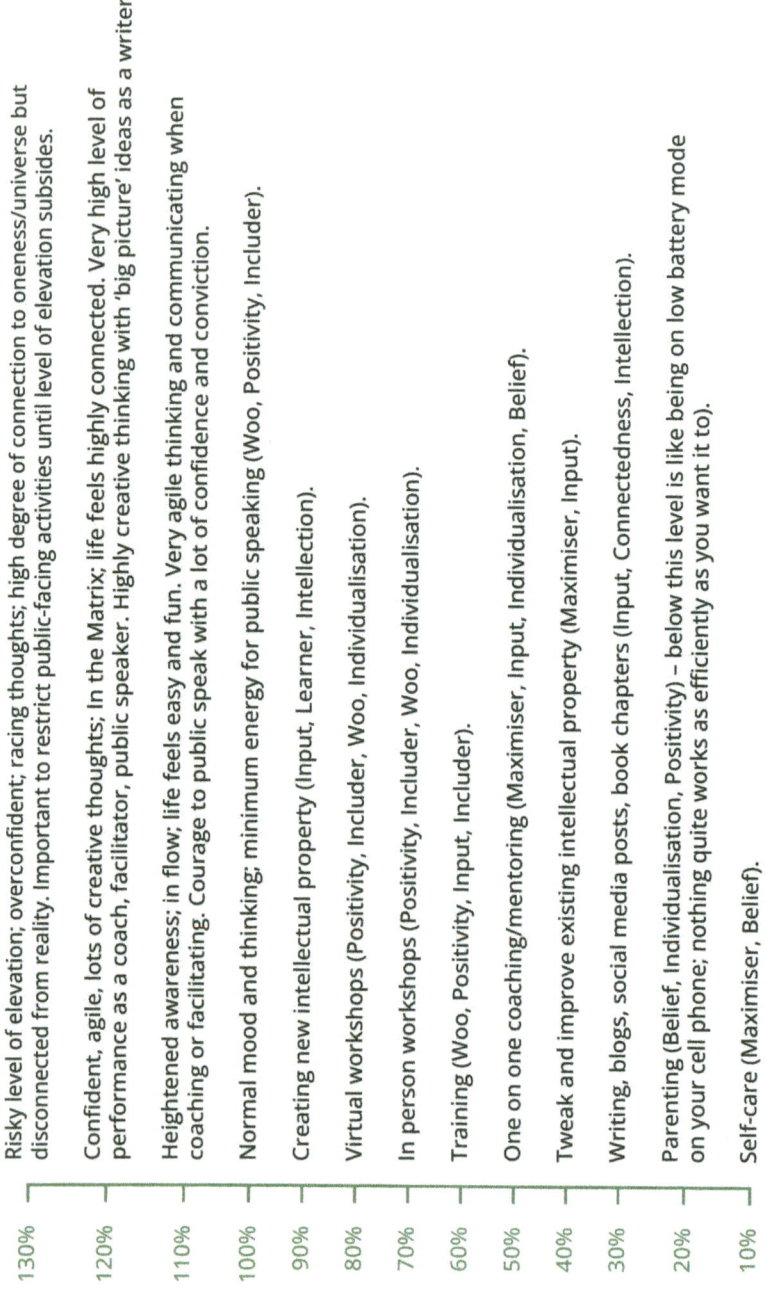

SUCCESS AND HAPPINESS...

Finding FISH in a Strengths-Based Practice

for competition, but normally support him from home. When I am in a stronger energy state, I take great pride and pleasure in travelling with him domestically or internationally to cheer him on in person at his events.

I am grateful that my energy and mood levels are most often in the 90 to 110 percent range, but my self-awareness using the preceding table means that I can function normally at most other times. I just have to be deliberately selective about what activities I prioritise on any given day. With practice, I can execute a high level of performance for the activities I love most or do best, even when energy or mood is compromised. Having energy above the 100 percent threshold is a gift that often appears in glimpses, but informs moments of 'superpowers' that, in retrospect, I find challenging to explain fully. These are moments that are nearly impossible to explain to someone who hasn't had a similar experience, and the closest thing in modern concepts is the 'flow state' coined by Mihaly Csikszentmihalyi. I have hypothesised that I might be able to modify my medication to increase the frequency and/or duration of flow experiences, though there is a huge personal risk to experimenting in this way.

How would your experience of fulfilment, inspiration, success, and happiness fluctuate with your available energy, and what can you do to maintain high levels of energy?

What 'big rocks' will you plan this year that will maximise your fulfilment, inspiration, success, and happiness experiences?

CHAPTER 10

Strengths-Based Marketing

*"The aim of marketing is to know and
understand the customer so well
the product or service fits them and sells itself."*

Peter Drucker

D)oug Hall, author of *Jumpstart Your Marketing Brain* and *Jumpstart Your Business Brain*, is one of my marketing heroes. I love the amazing depth of research he puts into quantifying the effectiveness of different business solutions, including marketing. I also love that most of his work has been done with small to medium sized businesses, so his theories are not aimed at corporate branding, but rather the positioning and marketing of your average small business (for example, a small motel in rural Prince Edward Island, Canada).

One of the principles he advocates heavily for is the creation of a Dramatic Point of Difference, a Blunt Overt Benefit, and a Real Reason to Believe, in developing a marketing platform. These can be described as follows:

- Dramatic Point of Difference – finding your uniqueness in the world; what makes you stand out from the crowd in a dramatic way.
- Blunt Overt Benefit – what results/outcomes/experiences do you create that are reliably delivered (and communicated in simple language)?
- Real Reason to Believe – what evidence do you have that backs up your Dramatic Point of Difference and Blunt Overt Benefit (for example testimonials, meaningful metrics, etc.).

To uncover the value in applying these concepts to a Strengths-Based Practice, we must explore how the strengths and talents of the practice owner their team express themselves through Dramatic Point of Difference, Blunt Overt Benefit, and Real Reason to Believe.

For example, given that Dramatic Point of Difference represents the uniqueness of the practice owner or of the practice itself, this could 'show

Finding FISH in a Strengths-Based Practice

up' as exceptional reliability and productivity (Get Stuff Done), a gift for entertaining and inspiring others, connecting deeply with clients or stakeholders, rigorous advanced thinking about an issue, or the magic of creating something completely new to address a client problem. The uniqueness, ability to create results, and historical evidence of the practice impact will be informed by the individual and collective strengths of the practice team.

The following table explores how each of the five categories of Strengths might be applied to each of these foundations in marketing. We then look at some examples from our interview content to show how each of the five Strengths categories may be used in a marketing context.

FULFILMENT, INSPIRATION...

	Dramatic Point of Difference	Blunt Overt Benefit	Real Reason to Believe
GET STUFF DONE	*How will your work ethic and productivity influence your Dramatic Point of Difference?* "Slowing down and having a more disciplined approach, whether it's social media, newsletters, or content for past clients or future clients." - Murray	*Why is your efficiency and reliable delivery so critical to your Blunt Overt Benefit?* "Lists become tasks to me, whereas emails are communication. And communication aligns with my top strength. So I asked my marketing consultant to email me one thing at a time, and I will answer." - Jennifer	*What metrics exist in the practice that you can build a reputation around?* "Spending coin on getting me in front of people that run podcasts, potential TV and radio interviews and lots of print. Every single week, I had one or two things that I was doing from a media standpoint." - Joe
INSPIRING yourself or others	*What sets you apart in the market and consistently dazzles your intended audience?* "I'm telling an inspiring story. That's my communication. LinkedIn ends up being marketing for me, because that's where I'm telling stories, so I get steady referrals from this big network." - Jennifer	*How does your ability to inspire play out in the creation of consistent outcomes for your clients?* "I'm actually really invested in fixing their issues and helping them get to a better place. Once I figure out a solution, I'm good at communicating it and bringing people along." - Anne	*How will you measure the impact of your inspiration with prospects and clients?* "Promoting the client with a group photo on social media. I want to highlight what a cool team they are and how they're strengths-based. Not in a marketing effort, more like a connection. The teams love seeing their photos out there." - Ty
CONNECT to the world around you	*Why is connection at the heart of your Dramatic Point of Difference?* "It's important to let people know what you are offering, because those are people who need it, and therefore they can get in touch, and yes, again, it's a win-win." - Vicki	*How does connection contribute to the tangible outcomes you deliver?* "There's a lot of barriers for people to understand art. My strengths, in terms of woo and empathy, give me the ability to talk to people clearly, and understandably. I'm a trusted starting point that allows them to have connection directly with artists." - James	*What evidence do you have of the impact of your connection or ability to connect others?* "Having webinars and conversations with people is what works for me. I have 15-20 minutes max of information to share, and then the rest of the time is questions, conversation, and curiosities." – Jo

Finding FISH in a Strengths-Based Practice

	Dramatic Point of Difference	Blunt Overt Benefit	Real Reason to Believe
THINK	What is the most dramatic and unique piece of intellectual property in your arsenal right now?	Why is the richness of your intellectual property essential to creating consistent outcomes for your clients?	How is the rigour of your thinking reflected as evidence that people can believe in?
	"I feel my strategic strength helps me see different options and audiences. That allows me to create a matrix. Would this piece of information be relevant? In what way do I tailor this? Input helps me gather ideas or examples from others that I can apply to my strategy." – Nicole	"I look at my particular marketplace and see who I'm best positioned to serve. I made a significant move from the US West Coast to the East Coast. Strategy allows me to see how I can transfer what I've been doing with technology people into pharmaceutical people." - Teri	"The marketing and business development parts come naturally for me. I give that same energy when I'm on stage with a group, and I always tell them, thank you for trusting me with your time and money. Those are the most scarce things we have in business." - Ty
CREATE something new	What new product/service/solution can you create that is dramatically unique in your chosen market(s)?	How can your unique offering deliver consistently higher or more reliable results than anything else in your market(s)?	What data do you need to collect about your new product/service to build evidence that can be used in the future?
	"I'm currently writing a book to share all my unique knowledge and experience on how to facilitate great team gatherings. I'm hoping this book will really help my ideal market - managers and leaders in the public sector - host more meaningful team gatherings themselves." – Antonia	"I built who I am and my business by teaching others how to market in a way that works for them. I was originally looking at just entrepreneurs, but what developed was a lot of strengths coaches trying to get started." – Jo	"I'll collect stories and case studies from people around how they've used some of the ideas and models I've shared. Figure out what's working well and share more of that." – Antonia

IN A LIFE WELL-LIVED 113

In reading the interview content, it is fascinating to witness so much self-awareness played out in different ways. Awareness that an individual is good at one approach to marketing, but not another, and building a strategy around that. Awareness of not being good at something and finding an outsource partner to compensate. Awareness that marketing efforts are in their infancy, and identifying future Strengths-Based strategies to develop.

The five categories of Strengths are also useful to consider a broad perspective when it comes to marketing. For example:

- GET STUFF DONE – why are your robust systems and consistent delivery so powerful in delivering your marketing strategy and tactics?
- INSPIRE yourself or others – how do you leverage your talent for powerful persuasion in the way you build your marketing messages and channels to market?
- CONNECT to the world around you – how are your powers to understand your audience so critical to your marketing strategy and tactics?
- THINK – how can you use marketing to become the thought leader in your field of expertise?
- CREATE something new – what can you create that would make your marketing efforts effective and easy to implement?

At the junction of Doug Hall's marketing paradigm and Thought Leadership lay additional insights. In the performance of think, sell, deliver, each of the marketing principles can shape practice positioning and clarify commitment to message, market, and mode (as explored in a previous chapter).

Finding FISH in a Strengths-Based Practice

	Dramatic Point of Difference	**Blunt Overt Benefit**	**Real Reason to Believe**
Think	What makes your intellectual property a unique contribution to your chosen market(s)?	Who has the potential to receive maximum benefit from your thinking?	What evidence can you gather that proves your idea offers significant benefits?
Sell	How will your unique perspective help persuade?	What promise are you willing to make and keep?	What benchmark data can you produce that will persuade your prospect to work with you?
Deliver	How will you communicate the uniqueness of your content during delivery?	What case studies will you use to demonstrate your key benefit(s)?	Who can you use to demonstrate the power of your product/service?

What aspect of marketing will bring you the greatest sense of fulfilment, inspiration, success, and happiness (FISH)?

Which of your strengths are most relevant to the creation and execution of your marketing strategy?

CHAPTER 11

Strengths-Based Selling

"Selling is not about convincing, it's about helping."

Unknown

AT THE HEART of any commercial organisation of any size is the art and science of selling. If marketing creates an interested prospect, or at least a prospect aware of your product or service, then selling is the conversion of that prospect from awareness to customer.

The strengths of the practice owner have a critical role to play in creating new customers, and these strengths may be very different from the talent they use to market the practice or deliver services. Selling is also the category of the practice that has the highest likelihood of being delivered in an inauthentic way, given the discomfort many people feel when selling. There is potentially an assumption that inspiring the buyer or influencing the buyer's motives is the most logical approach to selling, but this strategy only covers one fifth of the Strengths categories, and anyone with alternative strengths will feel inauthentic in delivering sales through influencing. There is power and effectiveness in simply adding as much value to a buyer by being yourself and leveraging both the seller's and buyer's Strengths profile during the sales relationship.

For example, selling from a position of 'Get Stuff Done' might emphasise the potential results of the purchase (save time, save money), or the reliability of the seller in providing information and keeping their promises become part of the buying experience. Similarly, a seller who leverages their talent for connection during the sales process will be naturally good at getting to know the buyer, expressing enthusiasm not just for their purchase motivation, but in their life and broader interests. They may also be particularly good at identifying the specific reason or personal pain that the buyer is trying to solve with their purchase. A highly technical sell might benefit from a thinking style of selling, with valuable and powerful models, or a detailed and explicit relationship between product or service features to benefits for the buyer. 'Create Something

New' may benefit from the energy of the seller in passionately explaining why their solution is unique or tailored to the buyer.

None of these styles of selling sit in isolation, and the seller will have multiple domains to sell from. The point is to lean into the categories of strength that come most naturally to the seller and perhaps avoid the categories that do not feel as authentic. We might also find an easy process to supplement (e.g. if you are not strong in 'Thinking', you might rely on practice material, brochures, recorded webinars, etc. to serve as the technical detail to supplement the sales process).

This chapter has been inspired in part by *Strengths-Based Selling* by Tony Rutigliano and Brian Brim and is also informed by *SPIN Selling* by Neil Rackham. These resources provide two of my favourite evidence-based approaches to improving the selling process and relationship.

As a starting point, it is worth considering the seller's style of selling according to the five categories of Strengths.

SELLER'S STYLE - TOP THREE QUESTIONS

Inspire yourself or others:
- How might you use your stage presence to wow a prospect?
- What compelling storytelling might you use to enhance the sales relationship?
- How can you create momentum and improvement ideas to solve your client's most important problem?

Think:
- How will you leverage your expertise and product or service knowledge to impress your prospect?
- What level of detail might be appreciated from your client?
- How will you think through your customer or prospect's greatest

problem or vision of the future, and how your service or product will help them find the right solution?

Connect:
- How will you use these themes to understand your client or prospect intimately?
- How will they know you care deeply about their success?
- What talents do you admire most in your client or prospect, and how will you let them know?

GET STUFF DONE:
- What promise can you make and keep with your prospect that will build some loyalty between you?
- How hard are you willing to work, and what resources will you orchestrate to help solve your customer's greatest challenge?
- What ethical principles will you proactively use to build your integrity in the eyes of the prospect?

CREATE something new:
- How can you create a customer experience through the sales process that delights the prospect in a way that makes it very difficult to say no to your offer?
- What progressive series of products or services can you create that would meaningfully increase the lifetime value of your customer?
- What relationship management system do you need to create to keep track and leverage all of your valuable prospecting meetings?

But the seller's style is only half the story. It becomes really fascinating when you consider the five categories of Strengths from the eyes of the buyer!

The buyer also has a preference based on their own Strengths profile. In most cases, the buyer's Strengths profile will not be visible to the seller, but there are clues from the sales conversation that might give direction. A buyer who cares about Getting Stuff Done will be focused on the results of a purchase in terms of saving time and money and will likely light up in the conversation when efficiency and productivity are discussed. A buyer who cares about Inspiring Others will potentially focus on reputation, image, and the way the purchase will enhance their impact on others (family, friends, colleagues, etc.). A buyer focused on Connection will care deeply about how the purchase will lift the important relationships in their life. For example, a home purchase might have the potential to save enormous time, leading to better quality time with family members. A Thinking buyer will enjoy the complexity of features and benefits, and perhaps understanding what is under the hood of the proposed solution. How does it work? Why does it work? What is the evidence? A buyer whose energy appreciates Creating Something New will love the latest model, the most advanced features, cutting edge, market leading, future focused product or service.

CUSTOMER/PROSPECT'S STRENGTHS

INSPIRE yourself or others:
- How will your product or service boost their reputation (ego)?
- How might your product or service lift your prospect's ability to influence others?
- Why is your product or service the perfect incremental improvement to their life or business right now?

THINK:
- What information does your prospect value and need in order to make a purchasing decision?

- How will your product or service make your prospect more of an expert?
- What problem or challenge does your product or service anticipate or solve?

CONNECT to the world around you:
- Who does your prospect trust and need to consult before making their purchasing decision?
- Who else might be included in the buying process?
- How will you make the decision to buy easy in light of your prospect's natural talents?

GET STUFF DONE:
- How do they perceive kept or broken promises?
- How will your product or service make them more efficient?
- Why are trust and values so important in the selling process?

CREATE something new:
- What outcome can you create together through the client on-boarding process?
- What can the prospect create in their own life that they would value as a result of your product or service?
- How is creating something new for your prospect/customer at the heart of your product or service selling process and delivery?

In most cases, the seller does not have the luxury of knowing the Strengths dominance of their prospect, and rather they need to focus on touching on each of the five categories of Strengths during the sales process to see what lights up the prospective customer. It may become clear that one or two Strengths categories matter more than the others, in which case the seller can orient their talent on delivering to those strengths.

The Relationship Grid on the following pages for Strengths-Based

Finding FISH in a Strengths-Based Practice

Selling may be helpful in orienting the energy of the conversation in a way that leverages the seller's strengths while honouring the buyer's preference.

The magic happens when the most effective selling style is matched to the buyer's most significant preference. The seller's style is a reflection of authenticity (less cringe) while the buyer's preference is an indication of how they like to receive information or what motivates them most in a sale. Keep in mind that both the seller and the buyer can occupy multiple categories of Strengths, and that isolating to one style or preference could be limiting.

For example, if a buyer's preference is Connection, the seller has five different approaches they could take in fulfilling the buyer's need for connection. If the seller leads with Getting Stuff Done, they can build trust and loyalty with the buyer by being reliable, keeping their promises, and earning the reputation that they do what they say they are going to do. If the seller leads with Inspiring others, they can use their storytelling and their natural charisma to foster a trusted relationship or future friendship with the buyer. When the seller and buyer both lead with Connection, there is the potential for a strong and lasting relationship based on genuine interest in each other's life and success. When the seller leads with Thinking, their goal will be to provide relevant and compelling information that has the potential to enhance the buyer's need for connection and relationships. And a seller that leads with Creating Something New will benefit from identifying how the new product or service will lift the buyer's network or deepen their most important relationships.

The power of this approach is that there is no single way to sell. There is variety in both the natural, most effective selling style of the seller, and variety in the way a buyer likes to receive information and their motivation for buying.

The list on the following pages offers insight about what topic or direction a fruitful conversation might take. It is important to be aware that both the seller and the buyer have preferences that fall into more than one of the five categories of Strengths, and that dancing around the grid is likely to bring the most benefit.

In order to craft rich and effective conversations, the following list of Strengths-Based selling questions might be useful. It offers some language to identify the energy exchange between buyer and seller based on the different categories of strengths:

STRENGTHS-BASED SELLING QUESTIONS (SELLER'S TALENT PERSPECTIVE)

INSPIRE yourself or others:
- What new momentum might this product or service bring to your prospect's life or business?
- How will the eloquence of your sales conversation positively influence the buying decision?
- How will your confidence in your product or service raise the potential for your prospect to buy from you?

THINK:
- What data or evidence will you use to sell your product or service?
- What anecdotes can you tell about the effectiveness of your product or service? Why is the development history relevant to your prospect?
- What information can you research about your prospect before the sales conversation? How will you make them aware of your efforts to get to know them and their business?

CONNECT to the world around you:
- Who else might be involved in the buying decision, and how will you secure an audience with each of them?

Finding FISH in a Strengths-Based Practice

	Buyer's GET STUFF DONE	Buyer's INSPIRE yourself or others	Buyer's CONNECT to the world around you	Buyer's THINK	Buyer's CREATE something new
Seller's GET STUFF DONE	Mutual achievement and efficiency	Promise to promote	Loyalty based on hard work	Work hard to gather data	Work ethic to build something new
Seller's INSPIRE yourself or others	Momentum to achieve more	High energy exchange	Energetic trusted friendship	Dazzling evidence-based storytelling	Create a compelling vision of something new
Seller's CONNECT to the world around you	Cheerleading achievements	Enhancing talent and energy	Best friend success	Building expertise	Create something new based on trust
Seller's THINK	Information to achieve more	Information to persuade	Information to connect	Expert exchange	Create something new based on intellectual rigour
Seller's CREATE something new	Create something new that lifts achievement and efficiency	Create something new that helps the prospect inspire others	Create something new that builds trust and relationships	Use data and evidence to prove the value of something new	Create something together that delights the prospect

- What natural talent do you spot in your prospect, and how might your product or service further enhance that talent?
- How can you become your prospect's trusted advisor?

GET STUFF DONE:
- How will your tenacity and work ethic influence your sales funnel energy?
- How might you juggle all of your prospect opportunities and consistently advance each one?
- Why might your principles and values be relevant to your sales relationships? How could you make this a Dramatic Point of Difference?

CREATE something new:
- What system can you create that would make the prospect experience seamless and value-added throughout the process?
- What can you create with the prospect together that results in a positive relationship commitment?
- How does your product or service enable the prospect to create something new in their world?

Here are a variety of examples and implications of seller's and buyer's perspective when it comes to aligning with strengths.

Finding FISH in a Strengths-Based Practice

Strengths Category	Seller's Perspective	Buyer's Perspective
CONNECT	"The salesmanship piece has been around my Connections. Selling what I do softly through the network." - Anna "I lead with Restorative, so I am naturally invested in fixing client problems and helping them get to a better place. My coaching style is not purist, but a blend of consulting and facilitating strengths-based solutions with clients. As a salesperson, I am good at communicating potential ways forward and bringing people along." - Anne "Generally, people don't like being sold to, and you don't like selling. It is about relationships, knowing yourself, and telling the other person how you can work with them and help them." - Murray	Desire to feel connected to the seller and/or how the product or service will enhance the buyer's sense of connection to others.
INSPIRE	"Once I figure out as to what I think is a solution, I'm good at communicating it and I'm good at bringing people along." - Anne "Woo is something that I would like to draw on a lot more. On a few occasions public speaking recently, I've been able to use one of my strengths very differently; now I focus on connection – I hear you, I understand you. I get how you're feeling, and now I will win you over." - James	The buyer's desire to feel inspired, and to enhance their ability to influence others. A product or service that enhances the reputation of the buyer.
GET STUFF DONE	"Selling happens through delivery, and building a reputation over time." - Antonia	A buyer's desire to improve efficiency or productivity. How will this product or service help me save time or money?

IN A LIFE WELL-LIVED

FULFILMENT, INSPIRATION...

Strengths Category	Seller's Perspective	Buyer's Perspective
THINK	"Ideation is a big part of it, and Learner – learning what's going on, knowing what people or other people are doing. Deliberative sits in the corner playing devil's advocate, saying, 'What about this risk?'. My vision strategy comes from this idea of creativity, learning and deliberative working together." - Holly	Buyer's desire for evidence, data and proof that the product or service has value. Ability of the seller to inform the buyer using relevant and compelling information.
CREATE SOMETHING NEW	"My strategy helps me focus on which people and which places and where I have credibility. So I created the map to hone in on what that is. My Maximiser keeps making it better. I try to stay on the map, and then I let Maximiser keep improving what I do in the world I've established." - Caren	Buyer loves the most advanced, most unique solution to solve their problem. Often categorised as 'early adopters' of a technology or product.

What aspect of selling brings you the greatest sense of fulfilment, inspiration, success, and happiness (FISH)?

Which of your most significant strengths will you leverage in building your sales process AND delivering a valuable sales experience to your prospects?

CHAPTER 12

Strengths-Based Delivery

*"Success is not the key to happiness.
Happiness is the key to success.
If you love what you are doing, you will be successful."*

Albert Schweitzer

IMAGINE THE JOURNEY of many artists and musicians who show an early affinity for their art form (painting, playing the recorder). Through their school years they meet inspiring teachers who give them exposure to an increasing array of options to develop their talent. They might experiment with different mediums (sculpture, water colours, oil on canvas) or musical options (singing, piano, string, percussion, wind instruments). If the student is encouraged by someone significant (usually a teacher or a parent), their talent carries through to high school where they perfect a mode of art, play in a band, sing in a choir, or perform in an orchestra.

In most cases, the student will invest in one form of art, or one delivery of music (single instrument) and get very good at that art form. Unfortunately, their genius is often lost when making career decisions toward the end of high school. A few will have the conviction to carry their talent into college or university, but many will be persuaded to invest in a 'safer' career path based on the perception that the fine arts is a crazy slog with risky returns. Wouldn't it be wonderful if everyone had the opportunity to follow their heart, pursue their passions, AND get paid appropriately for it throughout their lifetime? Too often, the head makes the decision instead of the heart, and this doesn't always reflect following a path that plays to an individual's strengths.

What is much rarer are the individuals whose talent transcends the mediums they choose to work in. Consider Michelangelo, whose works included sculpting, painting, poetry, and architecture, and whose talent we still revere today. In the music world, multi-instrumentalists of exceptional ability include Prince, Dave Grohl (Nirvana), and Anton Newcombe who is said to have mastered over 80 instruments. It is interesting to consider their **exposure** to various art forms at the right stages of development and how **transferable** their aptitude was to different delivery methods.

The same concept applies in the development of a Strengths-Based

Finding FISH in a Strengths-Based Practice

Practice. Inspired by *The Thought Leaders Practice* (Matt Church, Peter Cook, Scott Stein) chapter on delivery methods, this chapter explores various options available to a practice owner, and how those options are informed by the natural talent and strengths of the owner.

The Thought Leaders Practice identifies six primary modes of delivery which include speaking, authoring, training, mentoring, facilitation, and coaching. Based on my research with Strengths-Based Practice owners, it might also be useful to consider consulting (an over-arching mode of delivery that leverages all of the other modes) and care for others (especially relevant in healthcare practices such as medicine, dentistry, chiropractics, and physiotherapy). Based on all of these different modes, you can imagine a practice owner, through exposure and aptitude, developing their skill and talent across some of these options, and, in rare cases, developing a high level of competency across all of them.

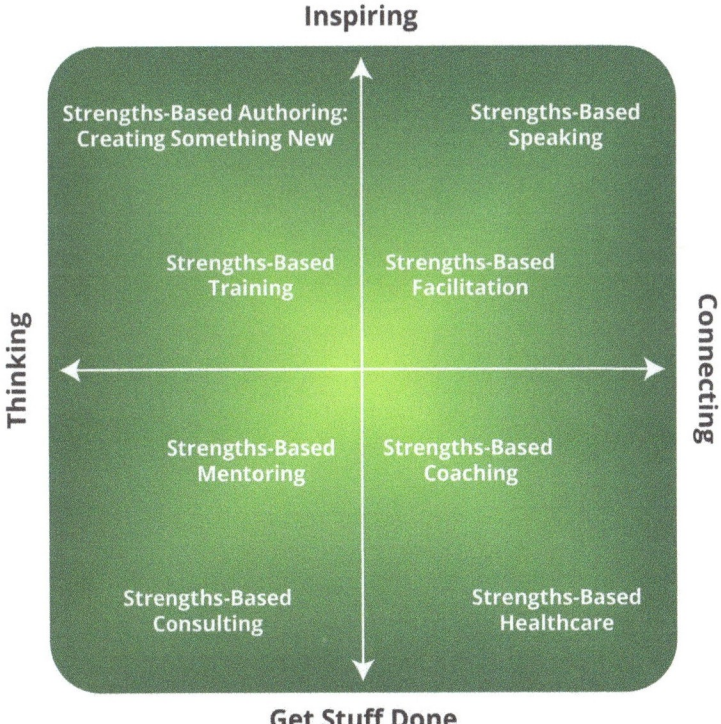

Based on this model, practice owners with different dominant Strengths profiles are likely to enjoy and excel at different methods of delivery, though there are always exceptions to the rule. And the irony is often that the method that seems most unlikely or is least preferred may have the potential to unlock something new commercially. The point of this model is not to select and lock in to a specific method, but rather to have the self-awareness in your abilities and preferences to experiment with many forms of delivery, especially the ones that play to your strengths.

Strengths-based healthcare is near and dear to my heart. During my MBA in Health Services Management in Canada, I had the opportunity to work in a teaching hospital, a pharmaceutical company, and a national laboratory / analysis company where I learned the power of people playing to their natural talent, both in leadership roles and in the care of their fellow human beings. This experience catapulted me into UK marketing roles in the pharmaceutical and biotech industries where excellence in management, team building, and understanding your customer/patient became cornerstones of leveraging the strengths of the people around you.

As I transitioned into business development coaching and management consulting in New Zealand, I retained my love of healthcare and had the opportunity to serve several dental practices, a national physiotherapy company, and the Ministry of Health. I am convinced that one of the keys to unlocking resource constraints and the tension between income, costs, and high-quality care lie in the implementation of a Strengths-Based Healthcare philosophy and framework. Time will tell how this might emerge.

One of my good friends, fellow springboard diver, and former client, Richard Greenwood of Discover Dental, offers the following observations:

Finding FISH in a Strengths-Based Practice

What are the benefits of a strengths-based approach in a healthcare practice?

One of the greatest benefits we've found as a practice is identifying where our Strengths deficiencies are. Most of our staff, including myself, are high in Empathy, and many of the other relationship building Strengths. Apparently, this is typical for a healthcare practice. Fantastic if you're wanting to genuinely care for people, but not so great if you are trying to develop and grow a business. Our team has a noticeable lack of strategic planning and executing strengths. This knowledge changed our recruitment criteria when searching for a new practice manager. And when we found someone, the result was remarkable. Suddenly we had this powerhouse of a person filling in all the weaknesses and voids in our staff skill set. It felt like the place was humming with the team functioning at a higher level than ever before.

Another problem with the high empathy or relationship building scores is the emotional commitment that staff make to caring for people, often at cost of their own wellbeing. We see many of the symptoms of burn out. But making staff aware of their Strengths and that they don't have to give their all, to every patient, all the time, helps them manage themselves better.

How do you leverage your strengths as a health professional, and separately as the practice owner?

Harmony, Empathy, Consistency, Developer, Learner.

My Strengths mean that I treat people the way I want to be treated, I never pressure or persuade patients to do things they don't want or need. I can put myself in their shoes and this helps me connect with them. We build authentic, trust focused/centred relationships.

As a practice owner I lead with a similar style, trying to keep everything fair and harmonious. This means listening to and considering everybody's points of view, and working very collaboratively with everyone in the team.

> *I'm also very interested in helping staff with personal development, spending a lot of time mentoring younger dentists. I recognise the satisfaction from learning (my Learner strength) but also enjoy helping others with their own education and growth (Developer).*

How would you describe your most powerful partnerships at work through the lens of strengths?

> *My business partner Ben and I have very similar Strengths, both have harmony and consistency in our top five. This means we work in considerate and caring ways to resolve problems and can trust each other to work towards a solution or outcome that is fair for all involved*

Richard's reflections are powerful in that they identify a dominant style of not just himself, but that of the whole practice, and when the right person fills the right roles (Practice Manager) lots of 'team deficiencies' can be compensated for, freeing up everyone to be the best version of themselves in life and at work.

Based on your current experience and aptitude, which delivery modes come most naturally to you? Which one are you most resistant to?

It is perhaps ironic that when we identify a delivery mode that we are reluctant to pursue, this may unlock commercial potential that cannot be achieved through the modes with which we are more comfortable. In my own case, I am resistant to training as a mode of delivery mostly because of my perception that it involves repetitive, non-creative delivery. But it is becoming more obvious that in order to bring more FISH philosophy to the world, training may be an ideal format to lift the skill of coaches, facilitators, and leaders or managers in the propagation of fulfilment, inspiration, success, and happiness (FISH).

Within the Thought Leaders community, it is common for practice owners to develop three or four of the delivery modes to a high calibre. Like my examples in music and art, there are a few individuals who have mastered most or all of the delivery modes through practice and aptitude.

Finding FISH in a Strengths-Based Practice

All of the modes have the potential to be world class. Your Strengths tell you which mode you're likely to be world class in. They are all as economically viable as each other.

While a specific Strengths profile might lend itself to a particular delivery mode (for example, 'Inspire yourself or others' lends itself to speaking), it is a powerful exercise to consider how every category of strength can be leveraged in each of the delivery modes. It brings to light the angle or perspective that a Strengths characteristic can bring to a given style of delivery.

Consulting:
- GET STUFF DONE – lean into substantial output in service of the client.
- INSPIRE yourself or others – create a vivid description of the change you will deliver to the organisation.
- CONNECT to the world around you – leverage your network to facilitate change.
- THINK – build data/evidence of the change you are creating.
- CREATE something new – create new structures, systems, and capability across the organisation.

Speaking:
- GET STUFF DONE – high commitment to a speaking circuit requiring work ethic and organisation; how will you orchestrate your current and future speaking events?
- INSPIRE yourself or others – energy to find the biggest stage where influence can be maximised; how will you keep track of your most inspiring content?
- CONNECT to the world around you – speaking based on a deep connection with the audience; how will you study and execute the art of deep connections with an audience?
- THINK – information-rich speaking with context and content

being well-represented; how will you filter your exceptional intellectual property archive to maximise impact with an audience?
- CREATE something new – build a unique experience for the audience to remember; what process or content will you create to make an event experience uniquely you?

Authoring:
- GET STUFF DONE – work ethic, rhythm, and discipline to write consistently; how might you leverage your productivity talent to maximise your volume of writing?
- INSPIRE yourself or others – harnessing the energy to pursue the dream of becoming a writer; who is likely to be most inspired by your writing?
- CONNECT to the world around you – connecting deeply with the intended audience; what authoring strategies can you use to consistently deepen your connection with your readers?
- THINK – writing process rich in research, data, evidence, and analysis; what new ideas are you courageous enough to share with the world?
- CREATE something new – transforming the writing into something tangible (book, magazine, documentary, training workbook, etc.); if everyone has at least one book in them, how many will you create?

Training:
- GET STUFF DONE – hugely reliable delivery with organised structure and dependable reputation; how will your talent for productivity and efficiency contribute to the training experience?
- INSPIRE yourself or others – creating a stage through storytelling and vivid imagery; how will you measure impact and transfer of knowledge or skill?

- CONNECT to the world around you – understanding the needs of trainees and flexing content to respond to those needs; how will trainees feel connected to each other and to the training content?
- THINK – training rich in resources, workbooks, models, and context; what is the cornerstone of your training intellectual property?
- CREATE something new – unique delivery formats that are memorable and impactful; what unique delivery style could you create that maximises impact?

Mentoring:
- GET STUFF DONE – working tirelessly for the mentee, with a high volume of value-add attention. What productivity lessons can you pass on and teach to clients?
- INSPIRE yourself or others – role modelling a desirable outcome for the mentee; who will your mentoring impact the most?
- CONNECT to the world around you – leverage your network for the benefit of the mentee; what experience could you share that would bring you and the mentee closer together?
- THINK – industry-specific information and models to help the success of the mentee; what's the most powerful metaphor you can think of that conveys your mentoring relationship?
- CREATE something new – create something with the mentee that delivers sustainable impact; what community could you create that might connect all of your mentoring relationships?

Facilitation:
- GET STUFF DONE – facilitators work ethic, structure, and organisation create a memorable experience; how will you maximise the efficiency of your facilitation engagements?
- INSPIRE yourself or others – magical moments are inspired

during the facilitation, coming from participants as well as facilitator; how will you measure the inspiration you create?
- CONNECT to the world around you – intimate connections are made between participants and with the facilitator; how will you facilitate deep connections between participants?
- THINK – a facilitator has a rich array of tools in their toolbox to facilitate events; how will the richness of content contribute to the impact of your facilitations?
- CREATE something new – unique experiences created for participants through content and process; what unique experience could you create that contributes to your reputation and positioning?

Coaching:
- GET STUFF DONE – reliable rhythm of coaching and wrap-around support; how can you maximise client numbers?
- INSPIRE yourself or others – consistent delivery of 'A-ha!' moments, energy, and momentum during the coaching experience; who will your coaching most inspire?
- CONNECT to the world around you – deep understanding and care for the client; what can you do to further deepen connection?
- THINK – coaching style rich in models and information supporting the client; how can you make sessions intellectually stimulating for yourself and your clients?
- CREATE something new – create a possibility or an option that was not available to the client before the coaching; what process or content can you create to make the coaching relationship deeply memorable?

Care for others:
- GET STUFF DONE – maximising efficiency in delivering care for others.

Finding FISH in a Strengths-Based Practice

- INSPIRE yourself or others – delivering inspiring outcomes for those in your care.
- CONNECT to the world around you – appreciating the ripple effect of the impact of your care on a wider circle of people.
- THINK – leveraging advanced technical knowledge in support of the care of others.
- CREATE something new – creating a unique service in the care of others.

In developing practice capabilities, consider a couple of different approaches:

- Within a delivery mode, expand the number and variety of strengths available to that mode, including leveraging the talent of everyone in the practice. For example, my dominant mode is coaching, and most of the statements above describing the various Strengths options that resonate with me, except for GET STUFF DONE which I rely heavily on my practice manager Tash for help with structure and organisation.
- Expand delivery modes while maintaining your Strengths categories. For example, you might be a great facilitator, partly because you know/get to know your participants so well, and have a wealth of insight about your chosen audience. This may be easily transferable into a speaking or authoring mode, where knowing the audience creates connection and positions you as an authority in their market.
- Combine delivery modes. Building interactive, highly facilitative public speaking adds richness and impact with an audience, and might combine speaking, facilitating, coaching, and training in one delivery. The definition of authoring can be very broad, and the powers of influencing through speaking become relevant when authoring a documentary, video training program, or podcast.

FULFILMENT, INSPIRATION...

The following interview excerpts demonstrate the prevalence of a particular delivery method or Strengths domain, with the identifying details removed. See if you can guess which method and/or domain are being described (answers follow on the next pages).

Domains:
Connect
Inspire
Get Stuff Done
Think
Create

Methods:
Consulting
Speaking
Authoring
Training
Mentoring
Facilitating
Coaching
Caring for others

Vicki

"A lot of my coaching is principle-based and – like you – energy-based. How do I bring energy to my clients? It's that incremental gain; how do we make this session a little bit better? How do we help you transform in this session so that you're a different person? How do we make you a slightly different person at the end of every session? That's my Maximiser at work.

Over many years of coaching, I've developed different tools, models, and examples. I have a repertoire of content I can share. I used to share everything all at once, but now I'm much more intentional about sharing the right piece of advice, model, or concept at the right moment in every session. I normally introduce only one or two pieces of information in any session. The rest of it is all energy and quality of questions. Sometimes it's a combination of knowing what not to say, and how one piece of information could transform a life."

Domain 1: _____

Domain 2: _____

Method: _____

Finding FISH in a Strengths-Based Practice

Marina

"When I'm listening, I notice if something doesn't make sense or if someone uses a word or a phrase in an unexpected way. This encourages me to explore the reason behind their choice of words. My relationship-building strengths guide me in deciding what to address, what to bring up, and what to explore further. Additionally, my love of learning and curiosity about people enhance this process."

Domain 1:

Domain 2:

Method:

Anna

"In my delivery, I focus on the relationship. How well am I connecting with my key stakeholder? A lot of the time, the way I do that is by leveraging my strengths. I want to satisfy my client or key stakeholder by providing them with interesting insights on the topic of relevance. It might be providing the latest thinking on cyber risk for an insurance client who is spending a lot on their cyber insurance policy. I proactively bring thinking to my client around working out the best way forward. For example, 'Have you thought about this? This could be a solution. This could be a way forward. How about we go down this path and then that focus piece which is the strength around staying on track?'"

Domain 1:

Domain 2:

Method:

Jo

"I will sit down and let people do their thing. I don't like intruding. So I'm good in front of the room. I'm good in smaller groups. I love smaller groups because it's easier to build conversation in a relationship, so I prefer smaller groups to larger groups. I tend to engage in conversations."

Domain 1:

Method:

Ty

"I like being on stage with huge groups; the bigger, the better. That's what I love, while for other people that makes them want to crawl in a hole! So I think there's space in all of this, no matter what you feel excited about or what method you want to play with, there are tons, and there are probably things that we haven't even come up with. Look what virtuals have done for us. That's opened up new things. There's a ton of room in this arena."

Domain 1:

Method:

Antonia

"I love creating energy in a room of people where they feel like they want to contribute more and share more and open up more. The energy I give helps them to connect. That's so easy for me to do. I think it's my positivity."

Domain 1:

Method:

> *Which delivery mode(s) do you suspect bring you the highest levels of fulfilment, inspiration, success, and happiness (FISH)? Do different delivery modes lift different elements of FISH?*
>
> *How do your strengths resonate with each of the delivery modes? Which strengths do you leverage most for your chosen modes of delivery? Are they the same or different?*

Answers:

Vicki
Domain 1: THINK
Domain 2: INSPIRE
Method: COACH

Marina
Domain 1: CONNECT
Domain 2: THINK
Method: COACH

Anna
Domain 1: CONNECT
Domain 2: THINK
Method: CONSULTING

Jo
Domain 1: CONNECT
Method: FACILITATE

Ty
Domain 1: CREATE
Method: SPEAK

Antonia
Domain 1: CONNECT
Method: FACILITATE

CHAPTER 13

Measuring the Practice and FISH

"Not everything that can be counted counts, and not everything that counts can be counted."

Albert Einstein

Stephen Covey famously coined the phrase "Begin with the end in mind" in his book, *Seven Habits of Highly Effective People*. This is important to keep in mind when considering what you want to experience by leading a Strengths-Based Practice.

- What legacy would you like to create?
- Who would you like to inspire? Why?
- Who would you like to become, and how much will you love the journey?

Before you begin measuring your progress, it is worth clarifying what is most important to you along the way. What would you like more of in your life? What would you like less of? The emotions you experience are as important as any material outcomes that might accumulate on the journey.

It is interesting to consider which of the four FISH elements (fulfilment, inspiration, success, and happiness) takes priority for you. Which one, when realised, leads to experiencing the other three? Every individual is different; I have had clients who lead with each one of the FISH elements in their lives, and experience FISH in a different order. Fulfilment is my highest priority, and when living my purpose, I find experiencing inspiration, success, and happiness effortless. When I am 'off-purpose' I can often descend in a downward spiral, with an absence of inspiration, success, and happiness.

Based on the premise that more FISH is a desirable outcome, it might be worth reflecting on the following.

- How might you measure fulfilment?
  - How clear are you about your Strengths-Based integrated purpose?

Finding FISH in a Strengths-Based Practice

- ▷ How easy have you made it to live your purpose every single day?
- ▷ Are your life purpose and professional purpose integrated or at least congruent?

🍁 How might you measure inspiration?
- ▷ Are you clear about your internal and external sources of inspiration?
- ▷ Do you have a repeatable list of inspiring experiences that you can tap into at any moment?
- ▷ How do you measure an inspiring versus an uninspiring day?

🍁 How might you measure success?
- ▷ When do you prioritise celebrating your achievements (personal and professional)?
- ▷ What financial measures might help you track your success (leads generated by marketing; sales meetings; proposals; $ sales; $ delivered)?
- ▷ What non-financial outcomes are worth measuring (client impact, lives touched/changed, connections, personal growth, intellectual property created, etc.)?

🍁 How might you measure happiness?
- ▷ How do you reflect and record what you are most grateful for in life and practice?
- ▷ What are your benchmarks for the happiest days in your life so far?
- ▷ How much variety do you have in your strategies for creating happiness for yourself and others?

In leading a Strengths-Based Practice, there may be value in recording your 'moments of magic' along the way. These might include life-changing feedback from one of your readers, creating a room full of raving fans at an event, facilitating deep connection and insight that moves one or more participants to tears, creating a product or service that changes a paradigm in an industry, changing the course of a life through a coaching series, building new skill or understanding through an inspiring training program, or providing compassionate care to someone when they are most in need.

One of the challenges is in identifying what to measure, or what currency we value in life and work. Measuring money, time, efficiency, and productivity is all well and good, but how would you measure the impact of a life-changing question during a coaching conversation? I am on a mission to discover the right life-changing question, for the right person, in the right moment – how do you place a value on that?

How might you quantify the experience of fulfilment, inspiration, success, and happiness? What if the ultimate measure of a life well-lived is the giving and receiving of love, in all its forms? Love of family, love of life partner, love of work, love of hobbies, love of home, love of country, love of the planet. What if the world found a way to measure and appreciate kindness, compassion, care, and love?

There is an argument that some emotions are difficult to measure because when we experience them we feel connected to something greater than ourselves that is immeasurable. Joy and love fall into this category, but they are both experiences that Strengths-Based Practice owners and their teams should cherish when they arise. I have speculated that FISH is not enough, and that perhaps we all need more JELLYFISH in our lives:

- Joy
- Energy
- Luck
- Love

Finding FISH in a Strengths-Based Practice

- Yes! (positivity)
- Fulfilment
- Inspiration
- Success
- Happiness

It is a powerful paradigm to do what you love with people you love in a way that you love (inspired by the Thought Leaders community) and I sincerely believe it is a standard that should become a human right, whether you are an employee or a business or practice owner. The world would be a better place for it.

MEASURING FISH (FULFILMENT, INSPIRATION, SUCCESS, AND HAPPINESS)

Finding FISH in a Strengths-Based Practice in time should feel easy and fun. If the practice owner and the practice team are playing to their strengths and doing what they love every day, fulfilment, inspiration, success, and happiness should flow effortlessly. Integrating life and practice will be essential to experiencing FISH consistently. There is no point in building a thriving practice if the rest of your life is in a shambles.

FISH questions to consider in measuring your life and practice include:

- What aspects of your life and practice bring you the most fulfilment?
- What are your sources of inspiration, both personally and professionally?
- How do you define success in a way that feels easy to live by and straddles your professional and personal life?
- What aspects of life and practice make you happy consistently? What are you most grateful for about your life?

One of the concepts being used and advocated for in sport more frequently today is the difference between an outcome goal and a process goal. An outcome goal might be to become the world champion in a particular sport, while a process goal might be to develop the best defensive system in the world and let in the fewest goals in the season. Process goals allow an individual or team to enjoy the journey and measure progress along the way without being overly constrained by the scale and magnitude of the outcome goal.

Insights from other Strengths-Based Practice owners include:

1) **Anne:**
   "I want to give other people that feeling I have of empowerment, of believing in myself. I want to help them be able to have that confidence and give it a go. So that is purpose."

2) **Michelle:**
   "We have conversations around fulfilment, inspiration, and happiness, all the time. We would probably not talk about success initially. Success, for me, naturally comes if you're making progress in those other areas."

3) **Julie:**
   "I have almost always experienced fulfilment, whereas I see success as the natural outcome, so it's always very important for me too. Maybe I don't forget about the happiness aspect, but I do neglect it."

4) **Lyncia:**
   "I'm always thinking, 'How can I help that person to be better? What do I need to do for this particular person to get what they needed from this interaction?'"

Finding FISH in a Strengths-Based Practice

5) **Teri:**

"It's easy for me to climb the next mountain and not take satisfaction, not bask in what I've already accomplished."

> *How will you measure fulfilment, inspiration, success, and happiness in life and in your practice?*
>
> *What role do your strengths play in achieving the measures for your practice?*

PART IV

Brightness of Future

"The future belongs to those who believe in the beauty of their dreams."

Eleanor Roosevelt

WHAT IS YOUR legacy so far in life?

What would you like your future legacy to be?

Inspired by Steve Jobs, what dent are you meant to make in the universe?

Every life has a profound purpose, and I believe our purpose is only revealed in the moment of passing from life into death. Perhaps you are meant to leave a legacy through your children, through your most loving relationships, or through your calling. The energy and courage to lead a Strengths-Based Practice offers an unbelievable privilege to do what you love, love what you do AND leave a lasting impact on the planet.

As you lean into your strengths, you will experience more moments of flow, and potentially oneness with the wider universe. If you are not so metaphysical, you will reveal strategies to fulfil your intentions more frequently and with more deliberate energy. I believe leading a practice is more than a job, and more than running a business; leading a practice has the potential to fully release your self-expression, deep down who you are, and who you are meant to serve.

Hopes and dreams are powerful motivators that can create progress and an energy of continuous improvement throughout life. It is interesting to consider the value and energy derived from hopes, dreams, goals, and intentions. Each of these has a different energy and purpose, and different people may excel at one or more of these powerful concepts.

A hope might be described as a feeling of expectation and desire for a particular thing to happen. You can be hopeful, but detached from the agency required to make a hope come true. There can be a feeling of leaving things to fate and that luck has a role to play in realising a hope. A lot of recent literature has devalued the power of hope. But, having lived the challenges of a bipolar life and lost my life partner to cancer, hope has kept me alive on more than one occasion. Hope offers something almost primal to cling to, and the belief that all of this has a bigger, more profound reason, creates perseverance to survive, cope, and eventually thrive.

Dreams, on the other hand, could be described as a cherished aspiration, ambition, or ideal. There is perhaps more commitment to a dream because it resides in the foundations of our wishes or expectations for our life. Rather than relying on luck, there is some implied effort needed to experience a dream or bring a dream into reality. Dreams can feel unrealistic or just out of reach, but the magic of dreams is the power of possibility. 'What if…?' is a favourite question of mine that often unlocks my own and my clients' potential. There is so much media around the law of attraction and the idea that dreams and thoughts CAN become reality. If you can dream it, you can become it. One of my mottos is to shoot for the stars, and if you fall short, you might reach the moon. The energy of visualising a dream, believing it to be true, and then experiencing it is the journey of creation.

Goals are more concrete in nature. They can be defined as the object of a person's ambition or effort – an aim or desired result. The details of a goal are usually more specific, and the more effective ones are time-bound in some way. The clarity of a great goal is often in its specificity and clear deadline. A goal offers a roadmap for a specific target to be completed. While goal-setting can be a powerful process, the idea that you have a future deadline to accomplish something can often result in delay, procrastination, and the failure of a goal to come true. This explains some of the limitations of New Year's resolutions.

Intentions are created by imagining the completion of a desirable outcome in a way that makes the achievement come true before you even start the journey. There is a certainty to an intention – from the creation of the idea, it is already true because you have seen the end result. An intention can also be described as the determination to act in a certain way, or a purposeful awareness of how you want to experience something. This is not far from the definition of manifesting. To fulfil an intention is to prove or to offer evidence of the accomplishment of some future desirable result.

Based on 24 years with my wife Fiona, intentions might be the most powerful of these four strategies for accomplishing things. While I lived a life of goal setting (mostly), my wife Fiona lived a life of intentions. She had a remarkable ability to visualise a future outcome and believe it to be already true. The best examples of this were when she sat across the breakfast table in Edinburgh with me and casually exclaimed, 'I know what I'm going to do before we immigrate to New Zealand – I'm going to cycle the length of Great Britain.' Now the irony of this is that although she enjoyed cycling, she was in no way doing the kilometres to justify this kind of achievement. Without a single pause in her energy, she proceeded to cycle around Edinburgh and up to St Andrews in a charity race, planned her route up the country, booked our bed and breakfasts, and, a couple of months before we left the UK, my three-year old son and I drove her to Land's End in Cornwall. She travelled solo for most of the journey, through sun and torrential rain. We dropped her off at the beginning of the day, and picked her up at a new milestone as she accumulated the extraordinary kilometres. We celebrated enormously when she passed from England into Scotland; the spiritual significance and the knowledge that if she had gone that far, she would surely finish the adventure. Following 17 days of effort, she rode into John O'Groats in Scotland with the satisfaction that she had made a dream come true.

That journey of self-confidence, effort and sheer determination made it easy for her to commit to another Greatest Imaginable Challenge: to complete a PhD. Her six-year journey of academics, interviews, research, and belief resulted in an amazing PhD in law that has set a precedent for children's autonomy in accessing health care which has the potential to change legislation worldwide. The most remarkable thing about her PhD was the fact that every moment, every milestone, every experience was a joy to her. Not one element of her PhD felt like a chore or hard work, and we laughed when we realised that the hardest thing about her

Finding FISH in a Strengths-Based Practice

PhD was the process of uploading the electronic file to the university's intranet! Her ambition to complete a PhD was born quite early in her academic and law career, and she was patient enough to wait for the right circumstances to allow it to occur.

While I lived a life of setting dozens of goals, and achieving 40 or 50 percent of them, Fiona only focused on one intention – one Greatest Imaginable Challenge – at a time, and all of hers came true. Food for thought.

It is interesting to consider how hopes, dreams, goals, and intentions work together to create a brightness of future in someone's life. In the time before technologically advanced navigation systems, a lighthouse on the horizon offered hope and safety to mariners trapped at sea for many weeks or months. The lighthouse provided a beacon to navigate towards, but also represented safe harbour, food, warmth, and reconnection to community. Similarly, hopes, dreams, goals, and intentions can provide a guiding light to navigate stormy waters. They provide clarity of direction, a roadmap for success, and a focus for where to direct effort, even if distracted by other priorities.

Perhaps a hope provides the initial stimulus to move from a current state to a future, more desirable state. Often a hope is irrational and feels deep in the soul, as opposed to in the brain or heart. A dream comes from the heart and represents the emotional motivation for a different future. Dreams represent what we want out of life and it is remarkable how many adults have lost the art of dreaming for themselves. Goals provide a framework using the brain – they are the substance behind the lighthouse, knowing that the light represents safe harbour, if the rocky shores can be safely navigated. For me, intentions are the most powerful of the four and might be the integration of brain, heart, and soul. They are the essence of manifestation – when you create an intention, you create a reality that has **already come true**. There is no possibility of failure. It is like being lost at sea, and visualising the reunion with your loved ones, no matter what.

What I know to be true is that hopes, dreams, goals, and intentions are irrelevant in the absence of actions. Whether through hope, a compelling dream, a well-thought-out goal, or a deeply fulfilling intention, change cannot be realised without an action. I often ask clients to take just one step, one action along the path toward an intention or a dream. Action creates momentum, and one action will quickly be followed by another and another. A Greatest Imaginable Challenge is simply the accumulation of many worthwhile actions in succession.

Often, the following questions help lift me from a funk or bring me new momentum in leading my practice.

- Hopes – what am I most hopeful for in the year to come?
- Dreams – what is the most important dream in my life right now?
- Goals – what achievement will I be most proud of at the end of this year?
- Intentions – what can I imagine having, being, creating, or experiencing today as if it has already happened?
- Actions – what can I do tomorrow to help all of the above come true?

A GREATEST IMAGINABLE CHALLENGE

One of my favourite strategies for motivation is to create a Greatest Imaginable Challenge. The inspiration for this was provided by an author previously mentioned in this book: Jim Collins. In his book *Good to Great*, Jim concluded that the very best companies in an industry shared a common visionary tool which he coined as their 'Big Hairy Audacious Goal'. The construct of a BHAG is largely relevant to big corporations, but it made me wonder if a similar concept might hold true down to the individual level.

Finding FISH in a Strengths-Based Practice

A Greatest Imaginable Challenge reveals itself at the junction of what an individual is most passionate about (in various aspects of their life), what they do best (better than 90 percent of the people they know), and where they can add the most value to themselves or others. Think of it as a Mount Everest to be climbed over the course of their lifetime, and different stages might emerge such as preparation for the expedition, accumulating the right skills and equipment, establishing base camp, forging staging posts, ascending the summit, and safely descending the mountain. A Greatest Imaginable Challenge is not meant to be easy, but it is meant to offer sustainable inspiration to keep making progress over a long period of time

To offer an example of a Greatest Imaginable Challenge from within my own life and practice, consider the following.

- Passion – helping lift FISH for practice owners in New Zealand.
- Do Best – Strengths-Based personal and practice development coaching and mentoring.
- Add Value – creating better quality of life AND more valuable practices for my clients.

Greatest Imaginable Challenge –
to meaningfully impact the GDP of New Zealand by lifting both the quality of life of business and practice owners and the value of the businesses and practices they lead.

Greatest Imaginable Challenges are not restricted to a person's professional life. My family and I are active members of New Zealand's springboard and platform diving community. Here is an example of a GIC within the diving world:

- Passion – for the art of falling with style,
- Do Best – organisational coach and cheerleader; event judge,
- Add Value – support Wellington Diving Club and the wider diving community.

Greatest Imaginable Challenge –
To use my business and personal development coaching skills to positively influence the Wellington and New Zealand diving communities to create sustainable high-performance internationally for more than a decade.

Other examples of GICs from my Strengths-Based Practice owner interviews include:

"I'd love to talk on the main stage at the strength summit in Omaha, instead of in a breakout room. That's a dream. I'd love to do that. I'd love to deliver the five-day global strengths coaching program. That's a dream I have for myself." - **Charlotte**

Finding FISH in a Strengths-Based Practice

"My business gives me the opportunity to support my family in a real and meaningful way. I've got four kids, my husband works super long hours, and I want to show my kids that a 58 year old can be out there still going after it, still believing in myself, still backing myself, still putting myself out there." - **Anne**

"I want to break down the barriers that exist in the art world. Art dealers are incredibly important, because they provide the opportunity to be a physical location for artists to showcase a body of work. I want to find a disruption model that helps artists and collectors. I'll do this by breaking down barriers in an industry that hasn't changed for 200 years, yet without damaging existing structures." - **James**

"My dream would be to be recognised as an expert or contributor. That's a big dream. I'll have invested a considerable amount of time and energy to achieve this, which is where the return comes from."
– ***Lyncia***

> *What Greatest Imaginable Challenge could you imagine that would feed your fulfilment, inspiration, success, and happiness consistently?*
>
> *How might your inspiration be lifted by the right Greatest Imaginable Challenge?*

Leaving a Legacy

*"Carve your name on hearts, not tombstones.
A legacy is etched into the minds of others
and the stories they share about you."*

Shannon L. Alder

REFERRING BACK TO the previous section, another useful perspective on brightness of future is to reflect on the legacy you intend to leave in the world, or, as Steve Jobs stated, the 'dent in the universe' you would like to make. Often, when people consider their legacy, they are future focused, but this is only a third of the story.

- What legacy have you created so far in your life? If you died tomorrow, what would you be remembered for – what would represent your past legacy?
- What legacy are you actively creating right now? What project are you working on that is not yet finished, but could be described as your current legacy?
- What future legacy do you dream of creating, and what resources or resourcefulness do you need to bring this legacy to fruition?

Various lists of the Seven Wonders of the World offer examples of legacies that have stood the test of time. Interestingly, as humanity has evolved, the various lists of different wonders have been developed. The Wonders of the Ancient World include the Great Pyramid of Giza. Those of the Middle Ages include The Great Wall of China. The Modern World Wonders include the CN Tower, and The Grand Canyon is one of the World's Natural Wonders.

These lists help in a variety of ways. They represent the greatest human-made and natural structures of their era, but they also imply that greatness evolves and changes with time, and that the dreams of humanity are realised in new ways as time passes. The same is true of a Greatest Imaginable Challenge. One achieved GIC builds on another, and each may be accomplished in a different timeframe. In fact, there may be substantial learning from a failed GIC that acts as the springboard to bigger and better achievements.

In leading your Strengths-Based Practice, what would you like your legacy to be? How many valuable and inspiring GICs can you create? Who will you impact and how will they remember you?

BEYOND A PRACTICE

As you imagine your future legacy and gain energy from your Greatest Imaginable Challenges, it becomes interesting to speculate about what comes after your practice.

The Thought Leaders community helps its members to crystallise a future after a successful practice has come to its natural end. If the practice's financial success has realised its potential, the practice owner should have savings and personal assets that allow for a comfortable retirement, if that is what is desired.

In many cases, a practice and practice owner reputation will grow in a way that leads to strategic partnerships or the launch of more traditional businesses that complement the practice owner's core positioning or intellectual property. One example of this is how Matt Church, the co-founder of Thought Leaders Business School, built a business from a long history of intellectual property development, and he maintains a black-belt practice as www.mattchurch.com, especially in the areas of speaking and leadership mentoring.

The evolution of a Strengths-Based Practice and the practice owner's body of work may transform from standing on the shoulders of giants to being a pair of shoulders to be stood upon. A huge amount of rigour, applied talent, and newfound wisdom are likely required on the journey to reaching this level of contribution.

The ripples that are created will often be unseen or unfelt because the impact of actions and intellectual property have hidden and unintended consequences. An interesting example of this came to me several years after I had been posting inspirational song lyrics to social media, sometimes with an interpretive comment, but oftentimes posting just the lyric. Unprompted, a connection of mine from a decade previously messaged me to let me know that my song lyrics helped her get through a particularly dark period in her life. I had no idea at the time, as she did not reach out to me during her difficult period, and I had forgotten that I even posted music lyrics! There was an overwhelming feeling of connectedness and gratitude to find out that I had created that impact.

The same ripple effect happens when someone is touched by our services, what we write, or what we say, and we may not find out for years (if ever) that the course of a life was changed. It takes courage to stand in your conviction knowing you are born to create an impact in the world, and trust that the universe will carry your message in whatever way it sees fit.

With love,
Christopher

Concluding Insights
by Lisa O'Neill

Christopher is very expansive. He has spent most of his life expanding people as a coach. His commitment to helping people to lead happy and fulfilled lives is everywhere. His experience and knowledge as a coach is impressive. I love how much knowledge this book has packed into it. Christopher has beautifully summarised some incredible bodies of work, combined with his own experience and expertise.

Helping people to love their lives, love their businesses and love their roles has been Christopher's work. His expertise, blended with life experience, is the perfect combination to expand into love. "Expansive love" is what the world needs and Christopher Miller is the right person at the right time.

Lisa O'Neill

WORK WITH ME

My Strengths-Based, heart-centred approach to leadership tends to resonate with clients who care deeply about themselves, their teams and the legacy they are trying to create.

I am always on the lookout for exceptional people to work with. I value authentic relationships that embrace the whole person, rather than just the world of work. My clients are like family, and I care deeply about their personal and professional success.

Typically, I work with business and practice owners and their teams of between 5 and 30 staff. In this capacity, I can get to know the individual strengths and talents of everyone in the business or practice to unlock the potential of the organisation.

I love mentoring Strengths-Based coaches and facilitators around the world to live what they teach and build commercial success for their practice.

Boards and executive teams of larger organisations often benefit from my programmes to enhance courageous purpose and values-based conversations that accelerate Strengths-Based culture change.

ABOUT THE AUTHOR

Christopher Miller holds a BScH degree in Life Sciences from Queen's University in Canada and an MBA in Health Services Management from McMaster University, Canada, where he was Valedictorian. His career journey spans the pharmaceutical industry in the UK, with roles at Schering Health Care Ltd (now Bayer), Invitrogen (now Thermo Fisher Scientific) and Pfizer, followed by a move to New Zealand. There, he supported business owners in strategic planning, business development and entrepreneurial mindset with Results.com, and worked for Gallup as a senior consultant leading employee engagement and culture change programs. In 2017, Christopher established his own Strengths-Based, Heart-Centred Leadership Practice, where he supports business and practice owners, CliftonStrengths coaches, boards and executive teams in their pursuit of exceptional businesses and lives through coaching and mentoring.

In his personal life, Christopher enjoyed a glorious 24 years with his life partner Fiona, before losing her to brain cancer in July 2021, a story he shares in his first book, *The Joy of Finding FISH: A Journey of Fulfilment, Inspiration, Success, and Happiness*. He lives in Wellington, New Zealand with his sons Cameron and Ross. When not serving his clients, Christopher can often be found cheering on his sons and judging the sport of springboard and platform diving.

Christopher is the founder of ExpansiveLove.org, whose purpose is to exponentially expand love on the planet through practical tools that lift love for individuals, couples, families, teams, organisations, and communities.

RESEARCH INTERVIEW ACKNOWLEDGEMENTS

Anna Charlton
Lion Consulting
Wellington, NZ
Top 10 Strengths: Learner, Strategic, Focus, Deliberative, Restorative, Intellection, Input, Achiever, Responsibility, Futuristic

Anne Lingafelter
ACML Consulting
Sydney, Australia
Top 10 Strengths: Empathy, Individualization, Positivity, Communication, Restorative, Woo, Competition, Focus, Activator, Futuristic

Antonia Milkop
Antonia Milkop Coaching & Facilitation
http://antoniamilkop.com
Wellington, New Zealand
Top 10 Strengths: Strategic, Developer, Achiever, Maximiser, Arranger, Belief, Activator, Responsibility, Positivity, Individualisation

Caren Leaf
Leaf Consultants, LLC
leafconsultantsllc.com
Denver, Colorado, USA
Top 10 Strengths: Strategic, Maximiser, Activator, Relator, Command, Individualisation, Achiever, Responsibility, Arranger, Self-Assurance

Charlotte Blair
The Strengths Partners
www.charlotteblair.com.au
Kyneton, Australia
Top 10 Strengths: Activator, Woo, Command, Arranger, Positivity, Responsibility, Communication, Maximiser, Individualisation, Significance

Holly Magnuson
Magnuson House Coaching
www.magnusonhouse.com
Covina, USA
Top 10 Strengths: Empathy, Adaptability, Relator, Harmony, Deliberative, Ideation, Arranger, Responsibility, Connectedness, Learner

James Blackie
The Art Counsel
www.artcounsel.co.nz
Wellington, New Zealand
Top 10 Strengths: Empathy, Ideation, Woo, Learner, Context, Adaptability, Positivity, Input, Arranger, Command

Jennifer Vancil
Communicating Strengths LLC
www.communicatingstrengths.com
Fort Collins, Colorado, USA
Top 10 Strengths: Communication, Connectedness, Maximiser, Woo, Relator, Positivity, Belief, Individualisation, Strategic, Ideation

Jo Self
Discover Jo Self, Practical Strengths
http://discoverjoself.com
Mexico City, Mexico
Top 10 Strengths: Strategic, Activator, Maximiser, Communication, Ideation, Woo, Arranger, Connectedness, Command, Positivity

Joe Hart
Joe Hart
joehart.com.au
Sydney, Australia
Top 10 Strengths: Adaptability, Relator, Individualisation, Learner, Restorative, Intellection, Strategic, Command, Analytical, Activator

Julie and Michelle, Hatch Talent
Michelle Burman and Julie Brophy
Hatch Talent Ltd
www.hatchtalent.nz
Canterbury, New Zealand
Top 10 Strengths:
Julie: Achiever, Learner, Input, Connectedness, Intellection, Futuristic, Focus, Maximiser, Self-Assurance, Developer
Michelle: Positivity, Woo, Input, Communication, Restorative, Individualisation, Includer, Activator, Strategic, Achiever

Lyncia Podmore
YOU Coaching
www.you.co.nz
Wellington, New Zealand
Top 10 Strengths: Strategic, Realtor, Maximiser, Arranger, Futuristic, Self-Assurance, Activator, Ideation, Adaptability, Positivity

Marina Mamshina
Marina Mamshina
mamshina.com
Sunnyvale, California
Top 10 Strengths: Individualisation, Strategic, Empathy, Connectedness, Learner, Futuristic, Developer, Maximiser, Relator, Ideation

Murray Guest
Inspire My Business
www.inspiremybusiness.com
Newcastle, NSW, Australia
Top 10 Strengths: Relator, Futuristic, Individualisation, Communication, Responsibility, Strategic, Positivity, Arranger, Woo, Activator

Nicole Weber
Quality Matters Consulting
Illawarra and Snowy Monaro, NSW
Top 10 Strengths: Futuristic, Strategic, Learner, Individualisation, Input, Ideation, Communication, Positivity, Relator, Woo

Richard Greenwood
Discover Dental
Discoverdental.co.nz
Wellington, New Zealand

Top 10 Strengths: Harmony, Empathy, Consistency, Developer, Learner, Analytical, Discipline, Positivity, Responsibility, Input

Sarah Blackie
Esby & Co
www.esby.co.nz
New Zealand
Top 10 Strengths: Learner, Individualisation, Ideation, Activator, Futuristic, Achiever, Belief, Developer, Input, Woo

Teri Johnson
Personal Best Partners, LLC
www.personalbestpartners.com
Chapel Hill, North Carolina, US East Coast
Top 10 Strengths: Strategic, Maximiser, Self-Assurance, Relator, Ideation, Connectedness, Communication, Individualisation, Arranger, Includer

TyAnn Osborn
Osborn Consulting Group, LLC
www.tyannosborn.com
Austin, TX, USA
Top 10 Strengths: Maximiser, Significance, Communication, Learner, Futuristic, Positivity, Input, Arranger, Self-assurance, Competition

Vicki Tipper
2BLimitless
https://www.2blimitless.com
Dubai
Top 10 Strengths: Maximiser, Positivity, Empathy, Woo, Developer, Adaptability, Connectedness, Learner, Includer, Context

Reader Praise for
Finding FISH in a Strengths-Based Practice

Christopher has written an excellent tool for reflection and inspiration. Drawing on his rich coaching knowledge and experience and that of his peers, Christopher takes the reader on a journey to consider and shape their practice, from inception to legacy. There is so much value in this book for coaches and anyone looking to take a strengths-based approach in their practice.

— Nicole Weber

Finding FISH is full of practical wisdom that is easy to apply. Christopher has provided examples, models, coaching questions and ways of looking that allow the reader to benefit in multiple ways. I resonated with what he said about feeling guilty when you get to do what you love most. He says, "Doing what you love most and playing in your passion creates an irony of guilt that may require unlearning, especially if you get paid to do what you love most." For the first 10 years of my professional life, there was no passion in my roles. Once I did create roles where I loved what I was doing, I felt a bit guilty for my life being so filled with joy. It took time with my coach and some reframing to realize how much of a gift my joy is to the world around me. Now, when someone says, "Wow, I wish I had your life!" I don't feel guilty, but inspired to talk with them about what, specifically, energized them about my work and lifestyle. I see it as an invitation to share.

— Teri Johnson

Finding FISH in a Strengths-Based Practice is a book brimming with wisdom, encouragement, a tonne of thought-provoking questions, and diverse strategies to help the reader establish and develop their strengths-based practice. Using the guiding principles of fulfilment, inspiration, success, and happiness, Christopher guides the reader on a journey to consider all the different aspects of building a practice that is founded on the strengths that light you up. It's a resource you'll find yourself returning to time and time again.

- Daria Williamson

Christopher's got this knack for weaving together different thought and personality models, creating insights that'll make you rethink your approach. Just like his first book, The Joy of Finding FISH, his latest, *Finding FISH in a Strengths-Based Practice*, throws out those 'aha' questions. Another one of his talents.

Understanding the nuances between hopes, dreams, goals, intentions, and actions has been so helpful for me. It's like having a trusty tool to constantly reassess what I'm aiming for. And it's not just me who benefits – it's going to be a game-changer for my clients too.

- Jason Biggs

Too often we focus on what we can't do or what we are not good at and give up. *Finding FISH* is an invitation to move beyond that and lead with our strengths for a life of even greater Fulfilment, Inspiration, Success and Happiness.

- Jet Xavier

In *Finding FISH in a Strengths-Based Practice*, Christopher Miller beautifully connects the concept of FISH (fulfilment inspiration, success, and happiness) to Gallup's CliftonStrengths methodology and numerous other exemplary works; emphasising the importance of understanding and leveraging our unique strengths to achieve success and fulfilment.

Inspired by the thought leadership of Matt Church, the idea of having a Practice, not a business, resonates deeply with the notion of building a venture that is rooted in purpose and authenticity. By viewing our work as a Practice, we shift our focus from mere profit-making to creating value, serving others, and continuously honing our craft. This mindset encourages a long-term commitment to growth, learning, and making a positive difference in the lives of those we touch. By integrating Gallup's CliftonStrengths framework with the concept of having a Practice, Miller encourages readers to cultivate a deep sense of self-awareness, embrace their strengths, and approach their endeavours with passion and dedication. This holistic approach not only fosters personal growth and fulfilment but also lays the foundation for building a sustainable and purpose-driven career or business. Overall, Miller's insights on linking FISH to Gallup's CliftonStrengths and advocating for a Practice mindset offer a refreshing perspective on how we can navigate our professional journeys with intention, authenticity, and a genuine desire to make a difference. It's a powerful reminder that success is not just about what we do, but how we do it, and the impact we create along the way.

- Helen Arthur

Christopher Miller's second book, *Finding FISH in a Strengths-Based Practice*, is an insightful guide on how to integrate personal strengths into business practices revisiting the framework of fulfillment, inspiration, success, and happiness (FISH). The book is well organised, beginning with foundational theories and progressing to practical applications for building and maintaining a strengths-based practice. Christopher's writing is engaging and filled with practical advice, backed by relevant research. He generously shares personal anecdotes and skillfully weaves together elements from various thought leaders, creating a comprehensive framework that is both inspiring and actionable.

The emphasis on the personal application of strengths to enhance professional life is particularly compelling, making it a valuable read for current or prospective practice owners and those interested in personal development within a professional context. Christopher's vulnerability and passion for helping others achieve a balanced and fulfilling life resonates throughout the book, making it not just informative but also motivational. He continually emphasises the potential to thrive by aligning one's business practices with what one loves, reinforcing the idea that there are abundant opportunities to create a successful business by doing what you love and loving what you do.

- Jo McIlroy

I felt very SEEN in your latest book *Finding FISH in a Strengths-Based Practice*. The descriptions of the dominant styles of leadership resonated for me, and perhaps help explain some of the challenges I have had as a people leader. By better understanding and recognising my natural talents, I have the courage to lean into my strengths and GET STUFF DONE and CONNECT to the world. Thank you!

- Nicola Millard

This is an extraordinary book, combining deep thinking with warmth, generosity and hopefulness. It gave me many ah-ha moments and provoked a deeper exploration of my own practice, purpose and legacy. With plenty of real-life examples, questions and practical tools, this book will challenge you but ultimately inspire and uplift you to find your own FISH in your practice. If you want a life well lived, you need this book.

- Linda Garnett

To use Christopher's words - the ripple effect of this book will be profound. This is a read packed with human insight, many ah-ha moments, and an amazing framework (FISH) for doing better work as a human, but particularly for those of us running a practice or business. In every chapter, there are questions, that if you take the time to read and work through answering honestly, will change, in no small way, the way you show up and do your work in the world. A must-read for anyone interested in doing their best work by playing to strengths.

- Alana Swain

Finding FISH in a Strengths-Based Practice by Christopher Miller is a comprehensive guide that delves into the practical application of strengths-based philosophies for both personal and professional growth. In this sequel, Miller expands on his initial concepts to explore how individuals can achieve fulfilment, inspiration, success, and happiness—collectively known as FISH—by harnessing personal and professional strengths. The book offers a robust framework for developing a strengths-based practice, enhancing professional relationships, and increasing workplace satisfaction. Miller's personal stories add a layer of authenticity and provide practical insights into utilizing strengths to navigate challenges and maximize potential. This resource is invaluable for anyone seeking to integrate the principles of FISH into their professional life and personal development.

- Susan Shaw

I run my own strengths-based coaching and facilitation practice and I loved the fact that this book covers a whole array of strengths tools and research. It helped me think about how to continue building my own practice based on various dimensions like marketing, selling and delivery and who I choose to partner with, based on strengths. After having read Christopher Miller's first book *The Joy of Finding FISH*, I highly recommend this sequel, especially for those looking to do the work they love using their strengths.

- Antonia Milkop

If you ask a dentist, a farmer, or an art dealer, 'Why do you do what you do?' they'll stare at you as though you're mad, as though you've asked an overly obvious question. But there are very few people on the planet who can clearly articulate why they do what they do. Not for an outcome, or income, but to reflect the reason you're on this earth. Chris has created this incredible handbook, walking you through these fundamental elements of business as they relate specifically to your strengths. Then he turns these fundamentals into a masterclass. In my early career, I genuinely felt spending time working on 'purpose' or 'values' was business navel-gazing. It took me years of working with Chris to unwind my ignorance, to see the benefits and reap the rewards. This book is a distillation of decades of Chris' wisdom and experience. And having the strengths lens turned onto business practices that include purpose and values, through to marketing and sales, means everyone who reads this book can develop a properly personalised program for their own business, and FISH life!

- James Blackie

Christopher's new book offers us a pathway towards a life where the realisation of our dreams leads to a future that is positive and fulfilling. Contained within these pages is an overview of practices interwoven with stories from people who have benefitted from a strengths-first approach. Drawing on his significant experience in running a strengths-based practice Chris presents us with the opportunity to craft a life in which "we love what we do, do what we love and inspire those we serve."

- Carolyn Stuart

Christopher's book is a practical masterpiece, a tool for all who seek to find their purpose and authenticity in serving others. His skill in connecting CliftonStrengths with other concepts and multiple life and work domains provides readers with tangible added value. The book also offers a wealth of essential questions, and a practical guide for entrepreneurs to reflect on their journey. Additionally, the shared integrated purpose statements of many strengths-based practice owners are a practical source of inspiration for those striving to define their own WHY.

- Ivan Kosalko

Through insightful exploration, Chris reveals the truth that doing what you love and excelling using your natural talents are the keys to sustained success and happiness in life, career, or business. Drawing from real-life experiences, he illustrates how a strengths-based practice thrives on the unique abilities of its team members, fostering an environment where Fulfilment, Inspiration, Success, and Happiness thrive. From cultivating self-awareness to leveraging individual strengths, this book offers invaluable guidance for both personal and professional growth.

I wish this book had been available when Julie and I started our strengths-based business 7 years ago! It's an indispensable guide to finding your true path and thriving in a strengths-based practice. Get ready to unleash your potential and embrace your brightest future.

Thank you Chris for another captivating exploration of the impact of strengths.

- Michelle Burman

Christopher Miller has done it again! In his second book, *Finding FISH in a Strengths-Based Practice*, he takes the concepts of Fulfillment, Inspiration, Success, and Happiness to another level for strength coaches who want to implement and frame their work (and their life!) around FISH. He provides a comprehensive review of FISH including how to measure it as a framework for his methodology of why running a practice is different than running a business. I found the concepts of FISH and the distinguishing characteristics of a practice to be foundational for how I want to grow my own practice.

He does an excellent job of helping the reader understand how our own strengths can and should be incorporated into how we operate our strengths-based practice with a thoughtful examination of integrated purpose, integrated values, partnerships, and leadership style as core entities of who we are, how we work, and how we live. Clearly, these are aspects of conversations we have with our own clients and therefore should also be infused into the way we run our practice. His words had me reflecting at a deeper level than I have before about my purpose, my values, and how I use them in my own coaching practice. He also provided encouragement for me to record and diagram how my strengths relate to my purpose and values for my own practice. He asks thoughtful questions (disguised as strategies) for identifying and saying out loud what really matters to me. Thank you for giving me the space to think about these things and more importantly a way for me to put them into action for my own practice.

For those looking for a road map on how to establish your own strengths-based practice, Christopher's book is a must-read. You will find the matrices and templates he provides on strengths-based marketing, selling, delivery, and measuring the practice of FISH as excellent tools for you to analyze your own talents and how they play a part in how you run your practice. He closes with an encouraging message about what legacy we want to leave. How to move forward after a trauma with questions about dreams, hopes, goals, intentions, and actions can bring new momentum and a renewed spirit. I found this chapter inspirational and a good motivator for me to elevate (and to activate on) my own desires to leave the world in a better place. Well done Christopher!

- Cheryl D. Lovell

Finding FISH in a Strengths-Based Practice is an enlightening guide that introduces the core concept that Fulfillment, Inspiration, Success, and Happiness (FISH) are integral emotions we carry within ourselves, not merely goals to be pursued. The book emphasizes the importance of self-awareness and regularly reflecting on how happy, creative, engaged, and purposeful we feel in our daily lives.

The book is rich with practical tools, thought-provoking reflective questions, and real-life examples that provide a roadmap for applying its principles. It includes personal resilience stories, emphasizing the importance of self-awareness and energy management in achieving personal and professional well-being.

Christopher Miller's generous advice and resources helped me deepen my understanding of how to integrate strengths into a living, breathing purpose that guides professional practice and enriches my personal life. These principles and tools are brought in this book, and it can be a great start or another step in your journey to personal and professional growth.

- Marina Mamshina

Christopher's book, *Finding FISH in a Strengths-Based Practice* offered impactful personal and professional insights which included:

- Strengths-Based Relationships: I immediately engaged in the complementary partnership exercise with my partner, incorporating our top 10 strengths with simple definitions. It has proven to be a great visual aid that sparks intriguing conversations.
- Strengths-Based Delivery: The matrix illustrating different delivery methods was a revelation for me. It has helped clarify my strengths in certain areas while highlighting areas where I may need improvement. Aligning with the strengths philosophy, I am motivated to explore all directions but focus on those that align with my strengths and bring tangible results.

I am looking forward to re-reading the book to gain even further ideas about how a strengths-based approach can lift my life and practice.

- Kristian Tudek

As someone who has built a successful Thought Leader practice and drawn extensively on CliftonStrengths to inform my work, much of what Christopher Miller writes about resonates with my experience. I know these principles to be true. But what rings even truer is Christopher's authenticity in presenting this material. He draws the reader into his own learning journey in a way that makes the content accessible and compelling. I know that he walks his talk — and it's that integrity that makes his encouragements in this book much easier to apply.

- Rebecca Sutherns

Pulling together real-life experience and many years of coaching, Christopher has created a guide full of purpose and inspiration. It's like having an experienced mentor at your disposal as you walk through the different aspects of a Strengths-Based practice. The contributions from other coaches and leaders Chris has worked with over the years adds to the knowledge and examples within the pages of the book. As always, Christopher has included thought-provoking questions to really get to the crux of what you are wanting to achieve. A comfortable read, that can be taken at your pace, and revisited as many times as you wish.

- Denise Mayhew-Leat

As someone who is working on building a strengths-based coaching practice, I found the chapter on Strengths-Based Thought Leadership incredibly valuable. The principles and frameworks around running a thought leaders practice are excellent as I seek to get clarity on my niche audience and messaging. The content of this book is gold for any strengths-based practitioner seeking to deepen their understanding of the work they love, and cultivate a more meaningful life and career. Kudos, Chris!

- Bryn Pane'e Burkhart

I was not really familiar with the Strengths-based approach until I read this book. Having run a successful business for over 26 years and a practice for four years, this book opened my eyes to what is possible. I wish I had read this book when I was starting out.

My advice would be please don't rush when you are reading this book. Christopher shares lots of powerful questions and it is worth having a notebook or device to capture your answers to his questions.

Exploring powerful topics such as purpose and values allows you to determine your own way forward. I love how Christopher also applies the strengths-based approach to areas such as sales and marketing. I love the diversity of the shares from the people he interviewed for this book. It shows how we are all different and how the strengths-based approach helps people to understand and work with their strengths.

I highly recommend this book. I especially appreciate Christopher's willingness to share his experiences and show how his life and purpose have changed over time. This is a book you should come back to many times as your life and practice change.

- Danette Fenton-Menzies

www.ingramcontent.com/pod-product-compliance
Lightning Source LLC
Chambersburg PA
CBHW041311110526
44590CB00028B/4322